D1384449

Emily Dickinson

═══════════

Le Dieu envolé by Camille Claudel.

Emily Dickinson

The Poet on the Second Story

JEROME LOVING

Texas A&M University

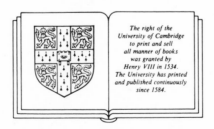

The right of the
University of Cambridge
to print and sell
all manner of books
was granted by
Henry VIII in 1534.
The University has printed
and published continuously
since 1584.

CAMBRIDGE UNIVERSITY PRESS

Cambridge

London   New York   New Rochelle

Melbourne   Sydney

Published by the Press Syndicate of the University of Cambridge
The Pitt Building, Trumpington Street, Cambridge CB2 1RP
32 East 57th Street, New York, NY 10022, USA
10 Stamford Road, Oakleigh, Melbourne 3166, Australia

First published 1986

Printed in the United States of America

Library of Congress Cataloging-in-Publication Data
Loving, Jerome, 1941–
Emily Dickinson : the poet on the second story.
(Cambridge studies in American literature and
culture)
Bibliography: p.
Includes indexes.
1. Dickinson, Emily, 1830–1886. 2. Poets,
American – 19th century – Biography.   I. Title.
II. Series.
PS1541.Z5L65   1986   811'.4   86–9617

British Library Cataloguing in Publication Data
Loving, Jerome M.
Emily Dickinson : the poet on the second
story. – (Cambridge studies in American
literature and culture)
1. Dickinson, Emily – Criticism and
interpretation
I. Title
811'.4   PS1541.Z5

ISBN 0 521 32781 4

To the Memory of My Mother

NANCY MacNEILL LOVING

If recollecting were forgetting,
Then I remember not.
And if forgetting, recollecting,
How near I had forgot.
And if to miss, were merry,
And to mourn, were gay,
How very blithe the fingers
That gathered this, Today!

Because I Could not Stop for Death –
He kindly stopped for me –
The Carriage held but just Ourselves –
And Immortality.

. . . .

Since then – 'tis Centuries – and yet
Feels shorter than the Day
I first surmised the Horses Heads
Were toward Eternity –

CONTENTS

PREFACE

On a June day in 1869 Emily Dickinson gave possibly the surest clue to the riddle of her life and work. She told Thomas Wentworth Higginson a "Letter always feels to me like immortality because it is the mind alone without corporeal friend." Higginson missed the meaning of the remark (which could have been easily quartered into another of her famous apothegms), and we as her future readers have missed much of her meaning ever since. She meant that her life and work combined to reveal what the poet John Keats called a "Cold Pastoral." The oxymoron derives, of course, from "Ode on a Grecian Urn." Dickinson listed Keats as one of her "Poets," and his phrase comes closest to identifying the voice we hear in her best poetry. Often posthumous, as in "Because I Could Not Stop for Death" (J. 712), it dwells on the forgotten promise of life much in the fashion of the scenes described in "Ode on a Grecian Urn." As Dickinson hinted to Higginson, the voice in her "letter to the World" was the sound of the mind fated to contemplate the dissolution of its "corporeal friend."

She had read, as she also told Higginson, Sir Thomas Browne and much preferred the metaphysicality of the seventeenth-century English poets to the "disgraceful" physicality of Walt Whitman, her American contemporary in the making of what Ezra Pound called the "new wood." But she wrote unlike Whitman's "master" as well, for Emerson had used "mind" and "soul" synonymously and seen the life as finally "whole" only when it was completed. As poet of the post–American Renaissance, Dickinson could not rely on either body or soul, but only on the "supposed person." This was projected by the "mind alone," or the disembodied voice whose claim to immortality rested upon perceiving the ratio between life and death. That voice remains for us today in the poems and letters Emily Dickinson wrote in the nineteenth century in her father's house on Main Street in Amherst, Massachusetts.

She wrote her "letter to the World," it should be remembered, on the second story; and we are not amiss to observe the double and often multiple meanings of such a circumstance, for the meanings of her poems are often as reclusive as the life she led. In both cases the sign over the stairway seems to read *Passage Interdit*. Her poems often keep as much out of sight as she did. Their themes reject or challenge the "first story" of Whitman's body and Emerson's nature as easily perceived correspondents of something spiritual. Her "mind alone" was never "in harmony" with either, for she knew that to become so – to focus on the beginning and end of life instead of its inevitable middle in experience – was to court the destruction of the "supposed person." In the poems her persona will "not stop for Death," but only for a life worth dying for. This was to be found in the "mind alone" on the second story, the subject of this book. It was suspended somewhere between the flesh and the spirit, beyond the talk "indebted to attitude and accent" and before the silence that absorbs individuality. Only the mind, or its poems, possessed – as she told Higginson – "a spectral power . . . that walks alone." It walked a fine line between life and death – or "Beauty" and "Truth," which we will remember from reading her poem on the subject, "talked between the Rooms" until the "Moss" had covered up their names (J. 449).

Dickinson wrote in the spirit and not the letter of the law which says that every existence has a beginning and an end somewhere outside the mortal coil. As in the case of Hester Prynne's letter "A" in *The Scarlet Letter*, her "letters" signified and authenticated the life in the here and now. In reading her today, we feel the "spectral power" of the woman who no longer exists. And yet the poems were just as disembodied in the nineteenth century as they are in the twentieth, for they issued from the mind that studied itself from the second story. It is little wonder that Dickinson's fugitive life has posed so many problems for biographers. Richard B. Sewall found the best solution or "key" to her mystery when he wrote first of the lives her life surveyed. Indeed, it was through this biography that I first saw the possibility of my own book on the elusive poet. Sewall's approach to her biography suggested a life hidden away on the second story of art. Her poetry, one might say, is made up of "sorties" over the lives of those around her, particularly those of her immediate family in the Homestead and in those of her brother's family living next door in the Evergreens. It is a psychological survey of those existences as they redounded upon her own on the second story.

Dickinson began her poetry on the first story, writing valentine's poems to possible suitors and girlfriends. In the earliest known exercise she writes that "the Earth was *made* for lovers," but even at this stage in her development (c. 1850) there is an awareness that the mad coupling of lovers ("Adam, and Eve, his consort, the moon, and then the sun") also includes "The *worm* [that] doth woo the *mortal*." From the beginning she includes the puritan *"application"* that despite her "reading of the roll" of lovers at all levels of nature, the addressee of the poem is nevertheless "a *human* solo, a being cold, and lone." Since this is a lover's or valentine's poem, however, he is offered the opportunity of enjoying the "happy, happy love!" of the two lovers described in Keats's ode. As Dickinson states the option in another valentine's greeting:

> Put down the apple, Adam,
>   And come away with me,
> So shalt thou have a *pippin*
>   From off my father's tree!   (J. 2)

Her father's fruit is not forbidden, and he may choose among six golden-red apples:

> There's *Sarah,* and *Eliza,* and *Emeline* so fair,
> And *Harriet,* and *Susan,* and she with *curling hair!*
> . . . .
> *Six* true, and comely maidens sitting upon a tree;   (J. 1)

The nameless one "with *curling hair"* is obviously Dickinson herself, who remains safe from the "harmony" of nature as long as she writes as the vicarious child of her father.

In other words, her retreat to the second story of her father's house allowed her to lock the camera eye on nature's possibility in the way Keats's scene on the Grecian urn freezes his two lovers at the height of desire. In both scenes the action stops short of consummation and fulfillment. Psychologically, Emily Dickinson never came down from the second story; she never left home to marry. Rather than join the pageant of lovers who passed under her window, she chose to "sculpt" them in their various attitudes and accents. What matured and advanced was not the father's daughter but the vicarious daughter of the father, the one who "acts out" in the poems the ratio or delicate balance between love and death.

An illustration of her theme is perhaps found in the work of another female recluse, the French sculptor Camille Claudel (1864–1943). Mistress of the more famous Auguste Rodin and sister of the Catholic apologist and poet Paul Claudel, she spent the last thirty years of her life locked away in an insane asylum. In her most productive years, however, she began to rival Rodin – with such now famous works as "Abandon" and "The Waltz." Her best known piece (because of its autobiographical parallel) and the one most suggestive of Dickinson's identity-theme is *Le Dieu envolé* (alternately called *L'Implorante, Implora-*

tion, and *La Suppliante*). Roughly translated as "The God Who Flew Away," the sculpture is a new and tragic version of Keats's ode. It portrays a beautiful naked young woman kneeling with hands outstretched. The object of her *imploration,* in the final variation of the statue completed years later, is a large male figure carrying an aging female on his back as he turns away. Claudel entitled the final version "Destiny" because it was her own to be rejected by Rodin after a fifteen-year love affair in favor of the older Rose Beuret, whom the sculptor eventually married. After completing her best work at the turn of the century, Claudel became reclusive and paranoid, convinced that Rodin was stealing her ideas for his creations. We will probably never know the extent to which Rodin was indebted to his competitor and lover. She was so convinced of his exploitation that she began regularly to destroy her works as soon as she had completed them. By 1913 she was considered insane by her family, who feared the social consequences of her erratic behavior, and – despite her repeated protests – shut her away for the rest of her days.

Full of pathos, it was her story as much as her art that drew record numbers to the Rodin Museum in Paris when an exhibit of her work was unveiled there in 1984. But the real story of Camille Claudel, like that of Emily Dickinson, is to be found on the second story of art. Looking at *La Destinée,* one sees the complex drama of humanity played through to its inevitable denouement. The kneeling lover has come so close to fulfillment and yet is already fated for disappointment. Imploring in vain, she is another of those

> . . . defeated – dying –
> On whose forbidden ear
> The distant strains of triumph
> Burst agonized and clear!   (J. 67)

The god departing is a victim as well because he leaves for old age, his passion spent and an old woman on his back. Sexless in her clothing, she represents the death of a scene that without her would become as pastoral with possibility as that of Keats in his poem. It was this possibility as seen in retrospect that became Dickinson's lifelong subject. In poem after poem we learn what might have been: Her life "had stood – a Loaded Gun" (J. 754) or had "closed twice before its close" (J. 1732). So much possibility and absolutely no probability. This was the object of her study on the second story.

Her argument with herself, however, is different from that found in, say, Whittier's sentimental poem "Maud Muller," because it focuses not on what "might have been!" but on the balance between success and failure. True "success" for Dickinson lay not in achieving the object of

one's desire but in discerning what made the object so desirable in the
first place. One could see so clearly only from afar, on the second story
of life. As she wrote:

> Success is counted sweetest
> By those who ne'er succeed.   (J. 67)

One had to lose in order to win.

The "winning" consisted of weaning the self of the first story in order
to write about it on the second. This is why the myths and legends about
Dickinson's life are important for an understanding of her poetry. Her
conduct of life in her father's house is full of suggestive contradictions –
scenes as oxymoronic as Keats's famous carving on the urn. The most
compelling is the fact that after thirty she wore nothing but white. Today
in her second-story room in Amherst, the visitor will find one of those
dresses hanging neatly in the closet. It resembles with its generous em-
broidery a rather simple wedding dress, as if the one "with *curling hair*"
were always about to join the mad coupling that Emerson called the
harmony of nature. In the poems this figure is always poised at the very
moment of heightened expectation. Like Claudel's kneeling supplicant,
he – or she – finds "success" in a "Cold Pastoral." Sculpture-like, the
poems freeze the various attitudes and accents of the human endeavor at
the point where life is always most intense. By this it is meant that the
poems address themselves almost invariably to the ratio between success
and failure, life and death – or what might best be described as the inevitable conflict between beauty and truth. Dickinson knew what Keats
knew: that beauty and truth are ultimately the same, because the first is
always to be consumed by the second. That was all we could, as he
warned, "know on earth." And *knowing* it meant comprehending the
ratio between the two.

This book is about Dickinson's success in appreciating failure. The very
paradox of that achievement has forced me to adopt something of her
"slant" perspective in order to get inside the echo chamber of her metaphors. Following the poet's own example, I have recombined Dickinson's life and art in the hope of demonstrating that the seeming disso-
nance of her words and images is really resonance, if not consonance.
My argument, therefore, is cumulative, if not linear, in its interiorized
approach. In Chapter 1 I begin at the end – or near it, in 1882 – and look
back on the life that Dickinson looked back on in her poetry. Her "second story" begins with the story of her brother Austin's extramarital
affair and the problems of commitment to love (and a lover) in the present instead of in either the undefinable past or future. For Dickinson,

experience was uroboric, and in this study I have sought to follow her
charting of it. Chapter 2 deals with our beginning in an unknowable but
nevertheless unforgettable past, and Chapter 3 deals with the end and the
inevitable arrival of the "hansom" man. The remaining chapters grow
out of this paradigm almost as organically as her poems grew out of the
realization that life could be fully experienced only in the subjunctive or
on the "second story." There her art became the "lie" that told the truth.
If this approach appears to be intuitive, it is to some extent. And yet the
careful reader will soon realize my indebtedness to the body of fine schol-
arship that precedes me. It has both schooled me in the wide range of
possibilities in her poetry and allowed me the opportunity to read that
poetry with the full seriousness it surely demands. By immersing myself
in the indirections of Dickinson's life and language, I have tried to experience the depth, intricacy, and (finally) concentricity of her "second-
story" point of view.

ACKNOWLEDGMENTS

As I stated in the Preface, it was Richard B. Sewall's biography of Dickinson that initially inspired me to write this book. That inspiration got
its first focus from a conversation (one of the many during his semester
visit to my university) with James M. Cox on the "second-story" aspect
of *The Scarlet Letter*. He also read one of my chapters and heard another.
Indeed, one particular fortune I had in writing this book was the frequent
opportunity to try out drafts of various chapters in this country and abroad.
At Dartmouth the poet Richard Eberhart told me a story that led to the
opening of Chapter 4. At the Sorbonne I received advice and encourage-
ment from Roger Asselineau and Giliane Morell. In Hamburg I got the
reaction of Charles R. Anderson, and in Vienna that of Waldemar Za-
charasiewicz.

Once again Norman S. Grabo read my manuscript. So did (in part or
whole) Paul Christensen, Mary Cameron Dezen, C. Carroll Hollis, Roy
Harvey Pearce, Kenneth M. Price, Vivian R. Pollak, and Susan Rober-
son. David Porter assisted me with both his *Dickinson: The Modern Idiom*
and his personal kindness. I thank Texas A&M University for a grant
during the writing of this study. Finally, I thank my wife and children
for their love, patience, and understanding.

Chapter 1

RUBICON

When Austin Dickinson wrote the word "Rubicon" in his diary for September 11, 1882, the act was far more symbolic than he probably ever realized. For Caesar the Rubicon had marked the point of no return in the conqueror's illegal entry into Italy in 49 B.C. For the brother of Emily Dickinson it marked an equally important and "illegal" juncture in his psychic landscape – the point at which he declared his love for Mabel Loomis Todd. At age fifty-two Austin was not yet ready to see himself, as his sister had written of those who had seen through the theoretical life of illusions, "As he defeated – dying." He was in love really for the first time, in love with love in the shape of a beautiful woman twenty-seven years his junior and, to make matters worse, the wife of a young instructor of astronomy at Amherst College. It was the first time he had felt this way since beginning what became his unhappy marriage with Susan Gilbert back in 1856. It was the first time, he thought with confidence, that he could define "Victory." This was doubtless the tenor of his conversations with Emily and Vinnie in the Homestead, a door away from his own. Neither sister could do anything but silently approve, for each had been disappointed by her "pseudo Sister." Yet it was Emily who saw the larger significance of Austin's determination to love a woman other than his wife, for it was this same need for "God's Adversary" that she had been trying to define in her poems.

Mabel had become Austin's "Christ," but the trinity was a *ménage à trois*. "*Do* be careful of this note," she urged Austin early in their relationship. "It frightens me when I think of your having it with you when you come home." Austin preserved most of her letters (with his own) but asked Vinnie to burn them after his death – "without opening." Fortunately, Vinnie was curious and the letters, unlike too many of Emily's, survived the fire. The correspondence reveals all the passion and high sentence we would expect from such an affair. But we can also manage with the distance of a hundred years the kind of objectivity Emily managed in her own observations of the pact. Doubtless, she saw the pathos long before Austin ever did.

Her brother had not experienced the thrill of "unselfish" love since the birth of young Gilbert, his third child, in 1875. Perhaps an unwanted child come late to Sue, a rival sibling to Mattie and Ned, Gilbert had probably awakened in Austin the same feelings Mabel was now waking. In both cases there seemed to be a rebirth of the spirit. But Gilbert suddenly died, barely a month after the first anniversary of "Rubicon." If Austin saw the loss as ominous, it did not outwardly affect his infatuation with Mabel. Emily, on the other hand, surely saw the import of Gilbert's death with regard to Austin's new reason for living. For the first time in fifteen years, she crossed the hedge that separated the two houses to console the child's parents. In a subsequent letter to Sue she described the eight-year-old as her "prattling Preceptor." This was not the first time she had used the word "preceptor – or its synonym "tutor" – so paradoxically. Apparently in reference to Benjamin Franklin Newton, a friend of her adolescence, she found the real lesson of life in his death: "I had a friend, who taught me Immortality – but venturing too near, himself – he never returned." Another "preceptor," Thomas Wentworth Higginson, taught her not by his death but by his (literary) deafness. He taught her, albeit unintentionally, that a poem had to be as ragged as life itself in order for it to approach truth. Gilbert's death was but another indication of the strange balance between success and failure.

The loss no doubt shook Austin's confidence in the possibility of a second chance in life, but he never got beyond the particular grief. Gilbert had simply left the life before it was over. It was Emily who could wade through that particular to see the universal pattern. She could see Austin's folly. Perhaps in Boston, now freed from Calvinistic gloom and guilt and in the heyday of Emersonian idealism or even Unitarianism, such an infatuation with life was worth trying. But in the Connecticut Valley, only a few miles from Northampton and the center of resistance to Arminian reform, it hardly seemed possible. Here in 1750 the great theologian Jonathan Edwards had been dismissed by his congregation for insisting that the quest for God's election begins anew with every day. Having succeeded Solomon Stoddard in the Northampton pulpit in 1730, he eventually tried to rescind his grandfather's compromise of the Half-way Covenant of 1662. No longer, Edwards argued, could church membership alone earn one the privilege of receiving the Lord's grace. "Mr. Stoddard's Way" was no longer the way to heaven.

Edwards had been a stern "preceptor," but his lesson was the same one Emily Dickinson had been relearning all her life. Indeed, no family in the Connecticut Valley had more fully absorbed it. Samuel Fowler Dickinson, the poet's grandfather, had absorbed it and so helped to found

Amherst College as an intellectual monument to the rigors of Christianity. The poet's father, Edward Dickinson, had absorbed it and thus did not think himself worthy of church membership until the age of forty-seven. "Presidents come and go," the Amherst saying went, "but Dickinsons go on forever." And so Austin Dickinson succeeded his father as treasurer of the college his grandfather had begun. But he was now refusing to follow what Jonathan Edwards, their first preceptor, had begun. With his Amherst "membership," he wanted the sacrament as well. Austin wanted a secular salvation – indeed, a secular trinity in the here and now. "I look after David – as part of my charge," he told Mabel in reference to her husband while she was abroad in 1885. "I think we three would have no trouble – in a house together – in living as you and I should wish." Sue was naturally excluded as the agony that made the ecstasy possible. She was the reason for this "pseudo-trinity" or triangle, and Emily must have seen the allegorical possibilities: Austin at the apex, Mabel and her husband at the feet. The condescension of it all seemed right for a Dickinson. In control not only of David Peck Todd's salary and chances for "tenure" but also of his wife, Austin Dickinson was turning the clock back to 1750, for the husband of Mabel, now a cuckold by Austin, was also a descendant of Jonathan Edwards.

Edwards, however, could not be cheated. No one in New England knew this better than Emily Dickinson, whose muse – like Melville's Ahab – walked on the legs of life and death. "I never lost as much but twice," she wrote around 1858. Ever since, readers have sought to identify two possible lovers – as if that would tell us any more about the meaning of the poem. Regardless of their names, the number could never exceed two, as Austin would learn from his *second* attempt at love. There was only one "affair" that allowed the lover to emerge with his illusions intact. Austin had already had it with his wife. The second time was the "second story," the fiction that tells the truth about life. It was Hawthorne's "second story" in *The Scarlet Letter*. "Twice have I stood a beggar / Before the door of God!" Hester Prynne might well have said. And with the statement she would have recorded, as Emily did, the full circle of experience – the "Zero at the Bone" that results from the attempt at a secular election.

What makes the Dickinson "second story" even more tantalizing is the fact that while Austin was pouring out his heart to Mabel, Emily was having her own "affair" with Judge Otis P. Lord. Indeed, as Richard B. Sewall tells us, "At least in this instance it is clear that Emily Dickinson was in love and that she was loved in return." Dickinson's letters to Lord confirm the fact of their mutual attraction, and there is even hearsay evidence that Sue Dickinson came upon the couple in a passionate embrace. Yet we can be fairly sure that the poet who had, vicariously or otherwise, already gone full circle in the lover's quest did not quite lose herself in the kind of romantic diction that Austin was exhausting on Mabel. Emily had already "scalped" her soul in the "Master" letters of the early 1860s. "Master," Otis Lord was not – her "church" perhaps for a time but never her "Christ." And so she could tell him in 1878, "Dont you know you are happiest while I withhold and not confer – dont you know that 'No' is the wildest word we consign to Language?" Far from Melville's "No! in thunder" (and indeed his fiction about Hawthorne's quarrel with God), it is as inscrutable as the White Whale itself, for "No" negated the "second story" – that fairy tale whose import was nevertheless true. Austin could not fall in love forever, but he could lose love forever.

There could be, in other words, no spiritual catharsis in Austin's symbolic suicide in "Rubicon." There was only life and then death, not life through death. This was the human condition, and in the face of it one could either retreat to the second story of the self or cling to the objective perceptions of the world. Emily chose the first while also mocking the second with her bridal-colored dress. Austin chose Mabel while also trying to people the void that his sister had already confronted in her poetry. He found in Mabel, he told her in a letter that reads more like a prayer or a confession of faith, a "perfect soul-mate, for time and eternity." Austin prayed to Mabel when he might have prayed to Jonathan Edwards. But Edwards had responded to Austin's notion of life with the wildest word we can consign to language; he had said no to his plea for life-in-life instead of loss-in-life.

Poetry

We know from Edwards's *Personal Narrative* (c. 1740) that he had learned early in life that religion or the quest for "election" had to be a solitary experience; else it was meaningless and misleading. Emily learned the same lesson. And like Edwards, who retreated to the woods and his "booth" to pray, Emily retired to the second story of the Dickinson Homestead – but to sing, not to pray. "Let Emily sing for you because she cannot pray," she told her Norcross cousins in 1863. She had indeed began singing the past two years, her strongest as a poet. No longer the victim of the kind of infatuation Austin would find in Mabel, Emily had grown even bolder than Edwards himself. As she told her cousins in the same letter:

> 'Tis not that Dying hurts us so –
> 'Tis Living – hurts us more –
> But Dying – is a different way –
> A Kind behind the Door –   (J. 335)

Living was in fact losing, and prayer – no matter how solitary – was an attempt to go "behind the Door" of such a life. It dwelt entirely on the "first story." Poetry, on the other hand, used the fiction of the "second story" to experience the first. Poetry was a way of dying without death. It rejected in its celebration of the tensions of life any and all notions of catharsis or redemption through death. It rejected the existence of a "heaven" as any more real or attainable than "success":

> Is Heaven a Physician?
> They say that He can heal –
> But Medicine Posthumous
> Is unavailable –
> Is Heaven an Exchequer?
> They speak of what we owe –
> But that negotiation
> I'm not a Party to –   (J. 1270)

Like "success" heaven was a "Medicine Posthumous," another oxymoron to explain the fate of the "corporeal friend."

Poetry celebrated the Fall of Man, that continuum of loss that forced Dickinson to come to psychic grips with the paradox of existence. It is in this context that we should read or reread her so-called "Master" letters. In doing so we might follow our example in the consideration of "I Never Lost As Much But Twice" and resist the urge to play the biographical guessing game. These letters, like her poetry, are not ultimately addressed to Samuel Bowles, Charles Wadsworth, or anybody else. They are dialogues with that elusive self whose identity or very conception depends upon the fact of death. As in her poetry, Dickinson engages here in the semiotics of survival: symbol hunting or myth making in the face of certain annihilation. In this sense there can be said to be an actual flesh-and-blood correspondent; yet his identity – like that of Mabel and Austin today – is finally irrelevant. Dickinson is singing to the self fated for oblivion: "As the Boy does by the Burying Ground."

It might be said that the "emergency" of the present never allowed this poet the luxury of transcendental correspondence with the other half "behind the Door." Unlike either Emerson or Whitman, she could not become "part or parcel of God" or render Him "the hugging and loving bed-fellow." The sights of her "Loaded Gun" were firmly set on the here and now – on that chimera known as experience. Rather than follow her American contemporaries in their celebration of man's "election" or her preceptor Edwards in his study of man's "damnation," ever and anon she strove to measure the ratio between election and damnation, life and death.

This sense of ratio animates her poetry, and our best introduction to her work is to be found in the "Master" letters. Three in number and addressed to an unidentified lover, they mark off the point where Dickinson first became seriously interested in writing poetry (1858) and the point where her power as a poet reached its zenith (1861–2). In the first letter we encounter experience in fragments, as it were. On the surface a "get-well" note, the underlying theme is the difficulty of shaking off the ennui of experience. The clue comes in the penultimate sentence: "How strong when weak to recollect, and easy, quite, to love." The desire to love stems from our relentless endeavor to *recollect* – to collect the fragments that were scattered with the "fall of man." She asks her "master" to instruct her in the rearrangement of experience. Where are the wings of love? Or, to put the matter another way, how can the "eye" repaint the "I"? How does the poet unlock the mirror image of experience, so that the two – the eye and its object – are once again correctly aligned? It was this paradox that she was beginning to study in her poems. An early one, written around 1858, shows that Dickinson was already concerned with the problem of recollection:

> If recollecting were forgetting,
> Then I remember not.
> And if forgetting, recollecting,
> How near I had forgot.
> And if to miss, were merry,
> And to mourn, were gay,
> How very blithe the fingers
> That gathered this, Today!   (J. 33)

Like the letter, this poem is on the surface merely another "get-well" message, in this case a valentine's sentiment (or note to accompany flowers sent). But the affection it speaks of is curiously described by its opposite. "How strong when weak," she writes in the letter. Man is strongest when weakened by the loss of living. He responds to the tensions it produces. Life depends upon the possibility of loss, recollecting upon the chance of forgetting.

   Reading the poem today, we cannot escape the sense that its voice is somehow disembodied. We are touched, perhaps, by the fact that its youthful owner has faded with the flowers she sent so long ago. The poem in one way is tied to the occasion of its composition: "How very blithe the fingers / That gathered this, Today!" But disembodiment was a necessary part of Dickinson's art. "You ask me," she told her "master" in the first letter, "what my flowers said. . . . I gave them messages. They say what the lips in the West, say, when the sun goes down, and so says the Dawn." In the subsequent "Master" letters and in her poems,

Dickinson refers to herself as "Daisy," the flower of love that dies in the West with a rhythm as punctual as the falling of the sun and the rising of the dawn. "The Daisy follows soft the Sun," the poet wrote in 1859:

> And when his golden walk is done –
> Sits shily at his feet –
> He – waking –finds the flower there –
> Wherefore – Marauder – art thou here?
> Because, Sir, love is sweet!
> We are the Flower – Thou the Sun!
> Forgive us, if as days decline –
> We nearer steal to Thee!
> Enamored of the parting West –
> The peace – the flight – the Amethyst –
> Night's possibility!   (J. 106)

This was Emily Dickinson's "personal narrative."

When Jonathan Edwards rode out into the woods to pray, he tells us, he "had a view . . . of the glory of the Son of God, as Mediator between God and man." He felt, he continues in an often quoted passage from the *Personal Narrative,* "an ardency of soul to be . . . emptied and annihilated; to lie in the dust, and to be full of Christ alone." The androgynous imagery in this "Second Coming" is hard to miss. Ejaculation and impregnation, or Christ as copulation, the "Mediator between God and man." But for Dickinson's persona the copulation is also the crucifixion. "You are my Christ," Austin had exclaimed to Mabel, but his sister knew that the transubstantiation of body and blood into ecstasy was but a dress rehearsal for the death throe. "One drop more from the gash that stains your Daisy's bosom – then would you *believe?*" she asks her "master" in the second letter to herself. Loving was the act of trying to *live,* but living required the slow death of crucifixion.

Disembodiment is the final result of the quest for love, and no American voice is more disembodied than Dickinson's. Recently, it has been suggested that Dickinson (as a feminist) goes beyond the nature of Emerson to "unnamable nature," that because God gave language to Adam and not directly to Eve, the female poet's muse must take her beyond the limits of language. The argument may depend more on critical tropes than textual evidence, but it is true that Dickinson pushed her "lexicon" to its limits. She nevertheless explored the same nature that Whitman, Emerson's poet, explored. Their achievements differ only in approach. It has been generally observed that whereas Whitman dilates, Dickinson compresses thought. But the differences run deeper than that. Unlike Whitman's persona in "Song of Myself," who is excited by the touch of his own body, Dickinson's persona is as disembodied as was the poet herself when her voice trailed down the staircase or from within the foyer to visitors to the Dickinson Homestead. It is somehow appropriate that we have a good many photographs of Whitman and only one of Dickinson – and this taken before she had become a poet. Dickinson's poetry is the poetry of disembodiment: "I'm Nobody! Who are you?" she exclaims, and there is no use in looking for her under our "boot-soles."

"If recollecting were forgetting," Dickinson is saying, we would be able to reach back to the wellspring of memory. Her poetry, as it were, speaks the language of oblivion. As with the narrative voice in *Moby-Dick,* Dickinson's voice becomes so disembodied that it might as well be the voice of God we hear. It is not the voice of the Christian god; as she tells us in a poem already quoted, "That negotiation / I'm not a Party to." Rather, it is the voice of memory. Her words go after the body, or nature, of course, but not exactly the body contained between her hat and boots. For Dickinson the body is better described in a Russian translation of Whitman's disclaimer about not being exclusively contained between his hat and boots: "a cloud in trousers." In this sense, she is the poet of the "mind alone," and not really the poet of the body – or the soul, for that matter. Her brother Austin was (at least in his infatuation) the "poet" of the body, but *her* heart, as she told her "master" in the second letter, simply outgrew the body: "Bye and bye it outgrew me – and like the little mother – with the big child – I got tired holding him." In her poetry we hear that heart ever trying to break through the silence of memory – the Pompeii of life's eruption so long ago. "Vesuvius dont talk – Etna – dont," she told her "master" in the second letter. "One of them – said a syllable – a thousand years ago, and Pompeii heard it, and hid forever." Dickinson's poet is always in danger of the fate of Pompeii, always in danger of a premature burial. Her poetry takes her to the brink of disaster, to the point where the body fails and the "eye" becomes the "I." It is as if she spoke that syllable of truth and, in a fitting epitaph to her existence in Amherst, "could'nt look the world in the face, afterward."

In a poem written about 1861 Dickinson wrote, "The very profile of the Thought – Puts Recollection numb." The closing stanza more than explains her preoccupation with recollection:

> The possibility – to pass
> Without a Moment's Bell –
> Into Conjecture's presence –
> Is like a Face of Steel –
> That suddenly looks into our's
> With a metallic grin –

The Cordiality of Death –
Who drills his Welcome in   (J. 286)

The word "nails" appears as an alternative for "drills" in the packet copy
of this poem, and it may make the statement more effective, for the fear
described is that the present negates our true identity in the irrecoverable
past and that we will pass nameless and without a "Moment's Bell" into
oblivion. No wonder Dickinson put so much energy into her "bookmaking" on the second story. Life for her was the act of recollection; it
was the attempt to tame the muse – the one who taunts her with the
possibility of a knowable past and who is indeed the addressee of the
"Master" letters. In this regard, the third and final letter is quite revealing. As Sewall observes, the first two "address a man to whom Emily
can speak eye-to-eye, but here she writes in abject humility, 'smaller,'
'lower,' an offender and a blunderer, not even knowing her fault." Here
we sense the exhaustion that creeps over her after recording in her poetry
a "love so big it scares her, rushing among her small heart – pushing
aside the blood and leaving her faint and white." The third letter records
the numbness finally brought on by such intense recollection. One is
ultimately turned back in his quest for "Rubicon." This letter marks that
point in Dickinson's development as both poet and person.

It is no coincidence that the poet's emotional crisis occurred at about this
time. Nor was it accidental that it culminated the period in which her
best poems were produced. The lives of the poet and the person had
finally converged on the second story. It makes little difference, of course,
whether the crisis involved a particular lover, as critics have suggested.
One or another individual would have inevitably produced the same effect: At about age thirty Dickinson simply hit the wall of experience. She
had already measured it in her poems and now had no place to hide, for
after the "second story" or loss in life, one looked not *for* love but through
it to the last illusion. It was a shotgun wedding of illusion and reality:

> Title divine – is mine!
> The Wife – without the Sign!
> Acute Degree – conferred on me –
> Empress of Calvary!
> Royal – all but the Crown!

Life was just possibly that kind of marriage – the act of being "Be-
trothed – without the swoon." Or "Born – Bridalled – Shrouded / In
a Day" (J. 1072).

This poem was written about the time of her crisis, and copies were sent to Samuel Bowles and Susan Dickinson, two of the biographers' and critics' candidates for the object of Dickinson's unrequited love. The search for the poet's lover began when her first books appeared in the 1890s. And despite the recent critical vote for a psychological "other" as the object of her intensity, the myth about a real-life lover persists. It survives because it contains, as all myths do, the germ of truth. No doubt Dickinson had a lover, or at least a "gentleman caller," in the late 1850s. Study of her early letters will bear out the fact that she entertained the expectations of a middle-class woman coming to maturity in Amherst society. It is not, therefore, wishful thinking to suspect that she enjoyed the normal adolescent experiences with the opposite sex – or either sex, for that matter. The important difference is that she learned from the experiences that each lover had to be embalmed in the memory of her songs in order for her to keep him. Indeed, he had to go the way of Homer Barron in Faulkner's "A Rose for Emily." It was the poetry of disembodiment that leaves not even that "long strand of iron-gray hair" the townspeople in Faulkner's story find after *their* Emily's death. Later in the decade, as already noted, she told Higginson, "A Letter always feels to me like immortality because it is the mind alone without corporeal friend." Only the lover's "spectral power" kept pace with the pace of one's experience. All else faded with the changes of time.

Faulkner surely knew the value of a myth. In the opening of his story the narrator tells us, "When Miss Emily Grierson died, our whole town went to her funeral: the men through a sort of respectful affection for a fallen monument, the women mostly out of curiosity to see the inside of her house." Doubtless, it was the same mixture of respect and curiosity that drew the townspeople of Amherst to Emily Dickinson's funeral in 1886. And the curious have been drawn in ever since, not to Amherst but to the poetry, which is haunted with the "spectral power" of their own experience:

> Pursuing you in your transitions,
> In other Motes –
> Of other Myths
> Your requisition be.
> The Prism never held the Hues,
> It only heard them play –   (J. 1602)

In 1884 Dickinson sent a copy of this poem to Helen Hunt Jackson, then the more famous Amherst-born poet, during her recuperation from a hip injury. One of her biographers suggests that the poem pays tribute to the "transitions" by which Jackson was recovering from her accident. It may also refer, he suggests, to the fact that Jackson was an endless traveler. Be that as it may, the poem also describes the mythological pull of Dickinson's poetry. That is, when we attempt to understand the Myth of Amherst, we pursue something mythological in ourselves. In search of meaningful experience, we find what Dickinson kept finding in Part Two of her life: that experience is inscrutable and can be understood only in the interstices of life. "Way leads on to way," Robert Frost would say a New England generation later in his own examination of the transitions in life. The poet in us all keeps discovering, as Dickinson describes it in the final lines of her poem, that life is a prism through which no light ever really passes. Our "requisition," our desire to know, "only *heard* them play" (my emphasis). The metaphor mixes sight and sound to articulate Dickinson's awareness – looking back from the 1880s – of what she was trying to accomplish in the poetry of disembodiment.

In order to understand the life and work of Emily Dickinson, therefore, we must stop looking for "facts" and listen again to her voice of experience. "Now I will do nothing but listen," Whitman finally decides halfway through "Song of Myself" – "To accrue what I hear into this song, to let sounds contribute toward it." This is what Dickinson set out to do at the beginning of her second half in life. She stopped looking for life and started listening to it. And what she heard was the song of the "mind alone." "Before I got my eye put out," she wrote in 1862,

> I liked as well to see –
> As other Creatures, that have Eyes
> And know no other way –

But if she could actually see all, she continues, the sky, the mountains, the meadows, or "As much of Noon as I could take / Between my finite eyes," she would still prefer sound to sight. For it is safer to *guess* "with just my soul"

> Upon the Window pane –
> Where other Creatures put their eyes –
> Incautious – of the Sun –   (J. 327)

Before she got her eye put out, Dickinson could think only of the first story, only of her flesh-and-blood self. Afterward, she could conclude her most famous poem by saying:

> Since then – 'tis Centuries – and yet
> Feels shorter than the Day
> I first surmised the Horses Heads
> Were toward Eternity –   (J. 712)

Elsewhere she would write that "Love – is anterior to Life – / Posterior – to Death" (J. 917). In other words, the flesh-and-blood love of the first story had to die before the "Life" of the poet began. It could return only after "Death" – when the disembodied voice could survey "centuries" of those transitions or interstices of experience. This voice could pass "the Setting Sun," or transcend nature's limitations. Really, it could and it could not, as Dickinson concedes in the next line: "Or, rather – He passed Us." The poet is always on the verge of sudden death, always about to control nature before it regains control of the poet, who is, as she says elsewhere, "Too near to God – to pray" (J. 716).

We will recall that she told her Norcross cousins, "Let Emily sing for you because she cannot pray." Her poetry lies on the very edge of experience – on the "Route of Evanescence" (J. 1463). Dickinson sent a copy of this poem to the Norcross girls. Composed long after her crisis years, it suggests the journey of the disembodied voice. Like the humming bird in "A Route of Evanescence," the speaker in Dickinson's poetry recedes from view. The voice alone remains – and through it, "The mail from Tunis [is] probably, / An easy Morning's Ride." What remains is the voice "That / Distills amazing sense / From ordinary meanings" (J. 448). The poet cuts through the ordinary to the mythological, and to understand Dickinson's contribution to American literature more fully we must do the same. We must confront the Myth of Amherst and learn how this "second story" informs the facts of her achievement as a poet.

Near the end of her life, Dickinson told a friend, "There is not so much Life as *talk* of Life, as a general thing. Had we the first intimation of the Definition of Life, the calmest of us would be Lunatics!" It is precisely that *talk* about Dickinson's that we must examine. In other words, why does the myth about her persist? Why does the general reader continue to embalm Dickinson in the image of abnormality? Why does the reader persist in believing that such a poetic vision was the result of a tragic disappointment in love? It was indeed the loss of love that made her a poet. But it was not the loss of one person; it was the loss of all persons. "Is God Love's Adversary?" she asked not long after another lover had passed through her life. If God was, the idea of declaring any kind of "Rubicon" was preposterous. Yet Austin Dickinson persisted and so made his sister's vision public: He made love to Mabel Loomis Todd, and Mabel as the poet's first editor made love to Emily. Without Mabel it is perhaps doubtful that we would have the poems at all. It is as if they are the offspring of Austin and Mabel's illicit relationship. The poems seem the fugitives from the society's myth that tried relentlessly to bury the real Emily Dickinson in the Pompeii of its own fears. Ironically, it was through just such a myth, Austin's "second story" with

Mabel, that we have Dickinson's "second story." What survives from her "first story" is a poetry that calls into account a life that is as elusive as the hummingbird itself. And the myth is part of this life; for without it there is no ratio to measure. The illusion of love, or life, makes the concept of loss possible. Austin's love for Mabel was but another example of the loss Dickinson celebrated in her poetry. Long after their tryst had ended and the two lovers had been put into the grave, the cuckold of this "literary affair" told his daughter it had ruined his life. Considered insane for the past twenty years and now institutionalized, David Peck Todd could do little more in 1939 than mutter some lines from this poem by Dickinson:

> I shall know why – When Time is over –
> And I have ceased to wonder why –
> Christ will explain each separate anguish
> In the fair schoolroom of the sky – (J. 193)

The poem was written around 1860 as Dickinson was coming into her strong period as a poet. Like Jonathan Edwards, Todd's forebear, she was then entering the woods to "pray."

Chapter 2

CALLED BACK

The tombstone for Emily Dickinson in Amherst, "three fields away" from the Dickinson Homestead, carries a most curious epitaph. Beneath her name and date of birth the legend reads, "CALLED BACK / May 15, 1886." This is the second monument to mark her grave. It was placed there in the 1920s by the poet's niece, Martha Dickinson Bianchi, who apparently chose "Called Back" instead of more traditional words, because it was the text of possibly the last letter the poet wrote – to the Norcross girls sometime in May. Although Bianchi doubtless interpreted the words to indicate the poet's expectation (and explanation) of death, Dickinson probably also intended a playful echo of the title of a book she had recommended to her cousins about a year before. In response to " 'what books' we were wooing now," she told them, "A friend sent me *Called Back*. It is a haunting story, and as loved Mr. Bowles [editor of the *Springfield Republican* and a close family friend] used to say, 'greatly impressive to me.' " Written by Hugh Conway (the English novelist Frederick John Fargus), the 1883 novel was widely popular in its day. What probably amused Dickinson about the potboiler, however, was not its sentimental plot but its use of blindness and amnesia. Its first-person narrator, Gilbert Vaughan, witnesses a murder without actually seeing it; his future wife Pauline sees the murder without actually witnessing (or remembering) it.

Briefly, the plot runs something like this. Vaughan, an Englishman who is temporarily blinded, enters the wrong residence at the moment a murder is being committed. He hears a young woman scream as the victim is being stabbed, then is captured and drugged by the murderers. Later he unknowingly encounters the woman, falls in love with her, and seeks her hand in marriage from her uncle. The uncle agrees only if the narrator will ask no further questions about her past. The woman, it becomes clear, is strangely aloof (having in fact suffered amnesia after seeing the murder) but is also obedient to her uncle's wishes. The subsequent marriage is naturally a strained affair, one the narrator cannot bring himself to consummate until his wife demonstrates her affection more overtly. The rest of the plot involves the uncle's incarceration in Siberia, the narrator's journey there to find out the truth about his wife's past, and the happy resolution typical of this level of fiction. In the course of the narrative, we learn that the victim was Pauline's brother and that he was killed by the uncle (or his henchmen) in an effort to conceal the embezzlement of the siblings' parental legacy.

The dilemma Conway presents in the subplot must have interested the woman who "never lost as much but twice." Vaughan must *see* and Pauline must *remember* if there is to be connubial joy. Each of them must be "called back" to witness the murder. In order to understand the poet's interest further, we might view the murder in *Called Back* as an allegory for the Fall of Man – that lapse into the state of amnesia called life. Although Bianchi applied the book title to her aunt's being called back to God, we are not amiss to view it the way Dickinson probably did. One was always trying to remember beyond the Fall – the "murder" that before time was had merged beauty and truth into a "Cold Pastoral." This attempt to see through the amnesia was the attempt to love. Through the act of love one tries over and again to remember. In the story Vaughan makes every effort to see the murder he has already heard. Appropriately, he succeeds only through his love for Pauline; that is, he finally sees it one evening as he holds his wife's hands in a clairvoyant exchange. His vision, naturally, has no more practical consequence than that of a dream, and hence to see or know the past empirically he has to travel to Siberia and question Pauline's uncle. Once he truly knows, Pauline regains her memory. The couple can now consummate their marriage, but it is also time for THE END in *Called Back*.

Life was the cyclic process of being called back from total ecstasy, and death was that one time when the call came too late. There is nothing left for Vaughan and Pauline to do but end their tale *and* their fictional existence. "My tale is told," Vaughan concludes. "My life and Pauline's began when we turned from that cemetery [where Pauline's brother is buried] and resolved to forget the past." Ironically, they resolve to forget the very thing that kept the story going and thus saved them from THE END. They are called back to nowhere but the oblivion that is the mainspring of every happy ending. "Just lost, when I was saved!" would serve here as a suitable epilogue. We encounter the same duality of fate that we found in "If Recollecting Were Forgetting." Remembering *is* forgetting, and once we remember enough to forget the past, we are finished. Trust must "dazzle gradually" or not at all.

Martha Dickinson Bianchi was not the only Dickinson to make sentimental use of Conway's title. Her mother Sue Dickinson gave "Just

Lost, When I Was Saved!" the title of "Called Back" when she submitted it to the *Independent* (where it was published on March 12, 1891). There is no doubt that the poet in this instance is being called back; however, it is not from death in the conventional sense but from the idea of death, the inevitability of which makes life a viable concept in the first place:

> Just lost, when I was saved!
> Just felt the world go by!
> Just girt me for the onset with Eternity,
> When breath blew back,
> And on the other side
> I heard recede the disappointed tide!

This is not a description of that rare brush with death but one that evokes the routine moments of a truly wakeful life. It describes the vigilant moments of one who is forever trying to remember by contemplating his dis-memberment – one who dwells on the edge of insight into the ratio between life and death. It evokes the rhythm of exhalation and inhalation, as he draws away from life and back into it again. Like Melville's Ishmael, the true poet is always going out and returning from the fatal voyage as the lone and lonely survivor:

> Therefore, as One returned, I feel,
> Odd secrets of the line to tell!
> Some Sailor, skirting foreign shores –
> Some pale Reporter, from the awful doors
> Before the Seal!

We can think of no paler "Reporter" in American literature than Emily Dickinson. The opposite of the ruddy Whitman, who maintains that "there are millions of suns left," she is always about to trail off into the silence:

> Next time, to stay!
> Next time, the things to see
> By Ear unheard,
> Unscrutinized by Eye –
>
> Next time, to tarry,
> While the Ages steal –
> Slow tramp the Centuries,
> And the Cycles wheel!   (J. 160)

Curiously, Bianchi and her mother made the same error through different approaches. Dickinson's niece applied "Called Back" to the notion that her aunt had died and gone to heaven. "Sister Sue" applied it to Emily's living and going to hell. Of course, Dickinson knew that one is finally called back from neither life nor death. He simply lives, as do Vaughan and Pauline, until the cycles of life "wheel" toward the HAPPY ENDING. Is there a more common and yet more provocative oxymoron than this one? This is indeed when the *"Wounded* Deer – leaps highest" (J. 165). This is "the Extasy of *death"* after which "the brake is still!" Nothing follows death but a crescendo of oxymorons – the stuff beyond the edge of space that the astronomer strives to contemplate: the "Rock that gushes," the "Steel that springs." Death is the HAPPY *ANDING* that brings sounds "By Ear unheard" and sights "Unscrutinized by Eye."

We might profitably take the metaphors suggested by *Called Back* into our inquiry of Dickinson's relatively early years as a great poet: 1858–61. It was about this time that she began to call herself back from society. To Sue Dickinson in 1859 she declined "an evening of amateur music" with girlfriends by asking her sister-in-law to "reserve an Ottoman for my Spirit, which is behind Vinnie's." By 1862 her seclusion was almost complete, but before that she was already testing the oxymorons of her "spectral power." "To live, and die, and mount again in triumphant body, and *next* time, try the upper air," she had already decided, "is no schoolboy's theme!" The problem as she began to perceive it was to follow the human spirit into the second story, to get beyond the body. This was not the same as seeing beyond the mortal ken, for Dickinson was as helpless there as the astronomy student. It was, as she said, "to live, and die, and mount again in triumphant *body"* (my emphasis). This was the disembodied body, and she began to seek out its possibilities in her solitary songs.

What was it to exist, anyhow? She would have agreed with Thoreau that "much is published, but little printed." Much was claimed for the life in society, but little or nothing was finally ascertained. None of the news was ever fit to print. Only in "broken Mathematics," she wrote, could "We estimate our prize / Vast – in it's fading ratio / To our penurious eyes!" (J. 88). In *The Four Quartets* T. S. Eliot called the future a "faded song, a Royal Rose or a lavender spray / Of wistful regret for those who are not yet here to regret." Dickinson is perhaps more to the point when she calls it a "fading ratio." Both are right, of course, in seeing the future as a reflection of the past. Otherwise, the future or death cannot be conceptualized. And so:

> As by the dead we love to sit,
> Become so wondrous dear –
> As for the lost we grapple
> Tho' all the rest are here –   (J. 88)

Life is defined for Dickinson, therefore, not simply by death alone but by the ratio between the two. It is found in the transition between life and death, which is, after all, what life consists of. Change is this poet's target, and it is an elusive, moving target. Later, at her zenith, she confesses that her life "had stood – a Loaded Gun" (J. 754). For now, it is more important to study that discovery as she makes it in her "penultimate" verse.

The first lines of many of her poems of this period suggest that the woman who confided to Higginson that she could not tell time until the age of fifteen had learned only too well by the age of twenty-eight. They introduced poeticized anxiety attacks: "A Day! Help! Help! Another Day!" (J. 42), "Could Live – *Did* Live" (J. 43), "If I Should Die" (J. 54), "An Altered Look about the Hills" (J. 140), "Dying! Dying in the Night!" (J. 158), "If I Should'nt Be Alive" (J. 182). They suggest the conventional fear of being called back from life – the fear of a premature burial. But this fear matures into a cosmic consciousness. The first "body" begins to give way to the second – to the disembodied body that will sit on the ottoman behind Vinnie. It is the body that lies "A Little East of Jordan" (J. 59). Here like Jacob, who sees God face to face and survives (in both Genesis 32 and Dickinson's poem), the poet survives by assuming the voice of the disembodied narrator. Like Vaughan in the story, she can now observe the "murder" with impunity. The important difference, of course, is that she does not try to verify the truth empirically or go full circle with the past. "I cant tell you – but you feel it," she observes in J. 65:

> Nor can you tell me –
> Saints, with ravished slate and pencil
> Solve our April Day!

"All the news," as we have noted, was simply unfit for print because it revealed that every day was All Fools' Day. Life was paradox, and one dared not publish without the certainty of perishing. It was better to remain back with the "mind alone" than to follow the "harmony" of the body to the end.

"Success," therefore, was always the knowledge of "succession" – never "Victory," – as she warns us in one of her most famous poems, "Success Is Counted Sweetest" (J. 67). The poem conjures up the agony of defeat in order to argue that no one can define "Victory" as well

> As he defeated – dying –
> On whose forbidden ear
> The distant strains of triumph
> Burst agonized and clear!

Anyone who confronts the clear truth must perish, becoming one of "the meek members of the [hoped for] Resurrection" – of those who are "Safe in Their Alabaster Chambers" (J. 216). "Alabaster Chambers" is more important to the Dickinson canon than even the poet herself realized. In fact, it was left to her sister-in-law to point this out. Emily sent several versions of the poem to Sue, and her response was exceedingly astute. After reading the second version she wrote in early 1861: "I am not suited dear Emily with the second verse – It is remarkable as the chain lightening [sic] that blinds us hot nights in the Southern sky but it does not go with the ghostly shimmer of the first verse as well as the other one." However, Sue did not favor either second verse, saying, "It just occurs to me that the first verse is complete in itself   it needs no other, and can't be coupled – Strange things always go alone." What Sue noticed about the poem is that nothing could realistically follow the moment of *safety* in the alabaster chamber or coffin. Dickinson's second stanza (in the original version) begins, "Grand go the Years." But the abiding suspicion is that nothing goes on for the observer after a confrontation with the last illusion. If the observer exists at all after death, the ratio of that existence to the life that remains is probably greater than that between an empire and a snowflake:

> Diadems – drop – and Doges – surrender –
> Soundless as dots – on a Disc of Snow.

Indeed, it was Dickinson and not Whitman who responded to Emerson's lament in "Experience." Whitman had responded to Emerson's self-willed optimism in the writings between *Nature* and "The Poet." Dickinson heard the later Emerson, the one who had already traveled (to borrow terms I have used elsewhere) from the poetry of vision to that of wisdom. Emerson was the precursor of Whitman's optimism and Dickinson's pessimism. Hence, in place of Whitman's dilated view of the friendly cosmos found in *Nature,* we have Dickinson's bolts of mockery in the face of the vanishing staircase in "Experience." It might be said that Dickinson completes the tragic vision that Emerson only dares to suggest in "Experience." After viewing man as a child eventually weaned of his illusions, he nevertheless insists that he finds "a private fruit sufficient." He clings to the belief that the particular is evidence of the whole. For Dickinson, on the other hand,

> "Faith" is a fine invention
> When Gentlemen can *see* –
> But *Microscopes* are prudent
> In an Emergency.   (J. 185)

Like another Emerson "disciple" in his more un-Emersonian moments, she displays her modernity by putting her "faith" in things. Like Thoreau, she trusts things or nature more than she does the "invisible wonders" it is supposed to represent.

Dickinson is the more un-Emersonian "disciple," however. And so it is easy to understand why she sent samples of her work to Higginson instead of Emerson. This poet was boldly mounting the staircase Emerson had ceased to climb. "Nothing is left us now but death," he concedes in "Experience." "We look to that with a grim satisfaction, saying There at least is reality that will not dodge us." In view of this resolve, really his version of "he defeated – dying," we cannot believe he would have greeted his "young contributor" at "the beginning of a great career." It is difficult to think he would have encouraged her to write poems of the sort she sent to Higginson in care of the *Atlantic Monthly*. Imagine, for example, the reaction of the author of "Experience" to "The Nearest Dream Recedes – Unrealized" (J. 319), one of the four poems Dickinson sent Higginson on April 15, 1862:

> The Heaven we chase,
> Like the June Bee – before the School Boy,
> Invites the Race –
> Stoops – to an easy Clover –
> Dips – evades – tears – deploys –

On the surface, the poem might be read as an echo of the fatigue in "Experience." But its disembodied voice is not discouraged by the elusive nature of reality. The voice of "Experience," on the other hand, is full of the body of Emerson, who is no longer "the novice I was fourteen, not seven years ago." He is no longer "youthful" enough to climb the stair of experience, but content to say, "Let who will ask, Where is the fruit? I find a private fruit sufficient." John Cody has argued that Dickinson's passage from adolescence to adulthood was abnormally slow – indeed stopped short of psychosexual maturity. But in terms of the poetry, the *poet* is quite "normal." That is, at her pinnacle she pursued the same thing the more "youthful" Emerson had in *Nature* –"The Heaven we chase."

What is abnormal about this poet is that she never averted her eye; she never wrote her "Experience." Just as she did not (or could not) follow her classmates into adulthood and marriage, as a poet she did not follow Emerson (and Whitman) from the heights of vision to the long plain of wisdom. Death never came to her "with a grim satisfaction." She never gave up her microscope in order to invent the fiction of "Faith." Had Emerson received the four poems she sent Higginson, he would have seen that she was simply incapable of making the passage. He would have seen with Sue Dickinson (in her observations on "Safe in Their Alabaster Chambers") that this poet was "safe" only when her eye was riveted to the reality of death. This *was* her vision. Unlike Emerson and Whitman, who are not finally elevated but rather deflated by the ratio between life and death and so retreat to the notion of nature as a "uniform hieroglyphic," Dickinson is satisfied with – indeed her poetic fancy is electrified by – nature as "the Missing All." Or, as she wrote in the third poem sent to Higginson:

> We play at Paste –
> Till qualified, for Pearl –
> Then, drop the Past –
> And deem ourself a fool –
>
> The Shapes – though – were similar –
> And our new Hands
> Learned *Gem*-Tactics –
> Practicing *Sands* –   (J. 320)

This is not the nature of Ahab's pasteboard mask, but neither is it the "Not-Me" of Emerson's *Nature*. Dickinson never allowed herself the safety of Melville's pessimism or Emerson's (early) optimism. For her the Not-Me is the real Me because it is the "mind alone." It is the only Me she ever works with. Her *"Gem*-Tactics" may drop the paste (which is an artificial way of putting things together, things like the "pasteboard mask"), but they never completely abandon the body for the soul. She is always "Practicing *Sands,"* making gems out of the mind instead of the soul.

Emerson had said in *Nature* that "the sun shines today also" – meaning that nature was ever prepared to minister to our psychological needs. To this Dickinson might have replied in the fourth poem she sent to Higginson:

> I'll tell you how the Sun rose –
> A Ribbon at a time –
> The Steeples swam in Amethyst –
> The news, like Squirrels, ran –
> The Hills untied their Bonnets –
> The Bobolinks – begun –
> Then I said softly to myself –
> "That must have been the Sun"!

The sun may be "but a morning star" to Emerson, Whitman, and Thoreau; but to Dickinson it is the only star. In other words, the meaning or the end is to be found in the transcendental means. Nature or the sun rises "A Ribbon at a time," but how it sets

> I know not –
> There seemed a purple stile
> That little Yellow boys and girls
> Were climbing all the while –
> Till when they reached the other side,
> A Dominie in Gray –
> Put gently up the evening Bars –
> And led the flock away –   (J. 318)

This poet is always the schoolgirl who is not at all sure how the sun sets or what the "harmony" of nature means. She persistently holds to that moment of youth and expectation in which, as we see in this poem, the setting sun is likened to "A Dominie in Gray" who leads her "flock" of children to evening study.

Much has been made of the trauma Dickinson experienced as she discovered herself unable to follow her friends and classmates into the commitments of adulthood. In most cases, marriage signaled the final separation, but the chasm between Emily and her compatriots first appeared during the teenage conversions to Christianity. By the early 1860s she had accepted her isolation as necessary to her vocation of poet and could even acknowledge an estrangement from her own family members, who, she told Higginson half-mockingly, "address an Eclipse, every morning – whom they call their 'Father.'" But the letters to her classmates in the late 1840s testify to the profundity of her initial fears. Under the weight of peer pressure at Mount Holyoke Seminary to declare Christ as her savior, she told her friend Abiah Root, "I feel that I am sailing upon the brink of an awful precipice, from which I cannot escape & over which I fear my tiny boat will soon glide if I do not receive help from above." It was fast becoming a solitary and lonely voyage. "Christ is calling everyone here," she told Jane Humphrey, "all my companions have answered, even my darling Vinnie believes she loves, and trusts him, and I am standing alone in my rebellion." The great lure of Christianity, of course, was that it offered an identity that abided life's inevitable changes – the gradual disappearance of childhood and adolescence. Yet it was an identity that also denied the promises of childhood and adolescence. With the coming of Christ, she thought, "something so desolate creeps over the spirit. . . . Heaven is seeming greater, or Earth a great deal more small." Christ's call, like that of death in her most famous poem (J. 712), was cordial at first because it offered salvation from the growing realities of existence. But it also made the Christian life that remained a bit stale, almost cadaverous. What remained were the waking dead: those who now willingly accepted life as a series of physical or earthly losses – as the body gave itself to the body of Christ. As Emily probably saw it, the first loss was that of virginity. First her female friends gave themselves to Christ and then to husbands. First Christ came to the psyche; then he returned in the form of so many *"boots, and whiskers"* and carried off her friends. It was the "Second Coming" that kept coming, and it was THE END as far as Emily was concerned. It simply ravished one promise after another that had been conceived in childhood and adolescence. As her friends surrendered themselves and deserted her, she turned inward, remained back as the vicarious daughter, and eventually wrote the poetry of the bridesmaid who never became the bride:

> I've heard an Organ talk, sometimes –
> In a Cathedral Aisle,
> And understood no word it said –
> Yet held my breath, the while –
>
> And risen up – and gone away,
> A more Bernardine Girl –
> Yet – know not what was done to me
> In that old Chapel Aisle   (J. 183)

Emotionally at least, Dickinson remained the virgin or the whole "person." This was not Emerson's Whole Man, however, because *he* finally required the example of Christ as the first Representative Man. The Whole Man of Boston, Concord, or Brooklyn was never quite as solitary as the Supposed Person of Amherst. There was one girlhood friend, though, who (despite the fact that she also heard "the Organ talk" and married) moved not away but next door as the wife of Austin Dickinson. Over the next thirty years Emily sent Susan Gilbert Dickinson more than 250 poems – overtures of a love that was more "spectral" than physical. The bridesmaid followed the bride into the bedroom, as it were. Daisy followed Dollie (Sue's nickname), and Austin found himself at the apex of his first triangle. Emily loved both of them dearly; yet it was through Austin that she made love to Sue. Through her brother, one of the band of *"boots, and whiskers,"* Emily was able to keep alive the promise of childhood and adolescence. Sue would remain, she hoped, her girlfriend for life. And life would retain its virginity and promise of ecstasy:

> A transport one cannot contain
> May yet, a transport be –
> Though God forbid it lift the lid –
> Unto it's Extasy!

> A Diagram – of Rapture!
> A sixpence at a Show –
> With Holy Ghosts in Cages!
> The *Universe* would go!   (J. 184)

Sue became the "girl next door."

Emily Dickinson had an almost obsessive concern for every member of her family. Sue was part of the family, but as the sister "a hedge away" she sang "a different tune" from the rest of the family members (J. 14). Before she had become a "sibling" she had become one of the sisterhood. As such she was the only one of Dickinson's inner circle of friends who survived the ravishment of Christ, or time. Through her marriage to Austin, Sue kept alive the tensions of life for Emily, the promise of love that Christianity (and marriage, its most effective institution) all but anesthetized. "Today is far from Childhood," the poet wrote in celebration of Sue's survival,

> But up and down the hills
> I held her hand the tighter –
> Which shortened all the miles –
>
> And still her hum
> The years among,
> Deceives the Butterfly;
> Still in her Eye
> The Violets lie
> Mouldered this many May.   (J. 14)

It was the survival of the sisterhood. Like the unconsummated marriage of Vaughan and Pauline in *Called Back,* the "wedding" of Emily and Sue could delay THE END. It could slow down the decay of time so well that even "the Butterfly" was deceived. Or as she writes of her liaison in the poem that begins "One Sister have I in our house, / And one, a hedge away":

> I spilt the dew –
> But took the morn –
> I chose this single star
> From out the wide night's numbers –
> Sue – forevermore!   (J. 14)

For Dickinson, more than for Thoreau, the sun was "a morning star." In 1858 and for a couple of years afterward, that promise of childhood

and adolescence allowed Emily Dickinson to write the poetry of the experienced virgin.

This is the poet who measures the loss of life through others; she lived
it vicariously through her Christ-ravished friends, then through Austin
as he acted as one of Christ's ravishers, and finally through Sue. This
"pseudo Sister," as Emily would later call her, acted out all the roles for
the poet: schoolgirl, Christian, wife, sister, and eventually mother. Sue
was the composite of one, the perfect *doppelganger*. Through her Dickinson was able to preserve her psychic virginity. Through Dollie she
could live without dying:

> Somebody run to the great gate
> And see if Dollie's coming! Wait!
> I hear her feet upon the stair!
> Death wont hurt – now Dollie's here!   (J. 158)

It was sex in the subjunctive, as Albert Gelpi has suggested in his reading
of the following poem:

> Wild Nights – Wild Nights!
> *Were* I with thee
> Wild Nights should be
> Our luxury!
>
> Futile – the Winds –
> To a Heart in port –
> Done with the Compass –
> Done with the Chart!
>
> Rowing in Eden –
> Ah, the Sea!
> *Might* I but moor – Tonight –
> In Thee!   (J. 249; my emphases)

Critics have been troubled over the physiological problems created by
the final two lines. When Higginson prepared the poem for the 1891
edition, however, he feared only that "the malignant [might] read into it
more than that virgin recluse ever dreamed of putting there." But Dickinson knew exactly what she was "putting there" when she used the
subjunctive. Here was the androgynous lover making love to Sue through
her priapic brother.

Dickinson's poetry, therefore, is a vicarious voyaging that probably
got underway with the marriage of Austin and Sue. It was through their

coupling that she first learned to resist the fatal flow of life. Her partici-
pation in it was always vicarious and thus real but never actual. That is
to say, it was no more actual than the activities Whitman celebrated as
"libidinous joys only" in the "Children of Adam" poems. Not long after
writing that series, he made the Emersonian discovery that "we exist."
Dickinson, on the other hand, always remained back before the ecstasy
and its consequence, the Fall of Man. Rather than allow the self to become mastered by the fit of creation – to become the "transparent eye-
ball" instead of the translucent eye – she stays "stock still" in her room
on the second story of life. Here began the poetry of psychic necrophilia,
where it is not life that is inseminated but the death that threatens every
pastoral. As "lover" her sexual acts were real because they were not actual. "Where are you off to, Lady," we might ask of Dickinson's persona
as Whitman does of the lonely but orgiastic lover in Section 11 of "Song
of Myself." Dickinson sets out to become the connubial partner of death
itself. And her poetry records their mating – or the ratio of life and death.

It is precisely her necrophilic approach to life, however, that keeps the
theme of death in the poetry from becoming maudlin if not sometimes
morbid. For the death throe resembles the throe that often leads to the
conception of life.

> A throe upon the features –
> A hurry in the breath –
> An extasy of parting
> Denominated "Death" –
>
> An anguish at the mention
> Which when to patience grown,
> I've known permission given
> To rejoin it's own. (J. 71)

One is "called back" through sex as well as death "to rejoin it's own."
The indefinite pronoun is important here, for Dickinson, as we have
seen, makes no clear gender distinction when she describes the act of
coitus. Men and women live the same way they die. And their sexual
"extasy" leads them to become "fathers" and "mothers" of life. In this
pursuit, the "ratio" between men and women is no different than the one
between the life throe and the death throe.

  Recently, feminist readings of Dickinson have attacked the "male"
metaphor for authorship in which the poet "fathers" a text. They ask, in
one of the most noted complaints, whether the pen is not a metaphorical
penis and wonder how the female artist creates literary offspring. But the

poet who always wrote as the "supposed person" would have scorned
the debate. She knew that the "extasy" of art required both sexes: the
male to "father" the text and the female to "give birth" to it. The poet
had "it's own" in both sexes, and so Dickinson's approach to life was as
androgynous as her involvement in the marriage of Austin and Sue. Rather
than commit herself to life in the first person of either male or female,
she held back as that androgynous third party who observed (and made
love) from the second story of art. Life was death in progress; hence, she
strove to have little *actual* to do with it. She remained the experienced
virgin, the poet who lives vicariously (like the twenty-ninth bather in
Whitman's poem) and is therefore not deflowered by experience. She
remained in the shadow of life, where the myth of childhood and adolescence was still a promise.

This was the only viable role for the poet at the end of the American
Renaissance. Emerson had come to his maturity when the dreams of
Washington and Jefferson were just being realized. "There is everything
in America's favour," he proclaimed in 1822 and began to prove it himself ten years later. Thoreau was the recipient of America's first educa-
tional fruits, a graduate of Harvard College a year after its bicentennial
celebration. Melville's faith in America was so strong (at least for a time)
that he could freely compare an American of Salem with the Englishman
of Avon. That American was Hawthorne, of course, and if he did not
think his talent comparable to Shakespeare's, he at least felt able in his
spare time to write the presidential campaign biography for Franklin Pierce.
Poe found time in his poverty-stricken life to bring American criticism
out of its relative infancy. And Whitman was an active politico in New
York City and Brooklyn long before he became the poet from Pauma-
nok. In other words, they could one and all afford to live up to Emerson's model of the American Scholar, for whom action was subordinate
but also essential. For the artist of Emily Dickinson's day, however, action was at best subordinate and finally baneful. Henry James's protagonists run out of psychic gas in both the New World and the Old. Mark
Twain's most memorable creation is forced to "light out for the Terri-
tory." William Dean Howells's Silas Lapham rises by falling. Kate Chopin's Edna literally exhausts the possibilities of the human condition. For
Stephen Crane's boy-soldier the "red badge of courage" is a fiction. Of
course, the fact of her sex in Victorian America imposed an additional
burden on our poet (and one that Chopin may reflect in *The Awakening*).
But the restriction went far deeper than that, not being limited to female
writers. At the end of the 1850s and on the eve of the Civil War, this
poet found herself in another country – in a place different from the na-
tional environment that had produced in the first half of the decade such

self-reliant statements as *The Scarlet Letter, Moby-Dick, Walden,* and *Leaves of Grass.* The America into which her genius awoke had already lost its virginity to experience.

Action was not now possible for the American Scholar. Only psychic necrophilia remained for the artist. America was, on the eve of war, about to become Whitman's suicide sprawled "on the bloody floor of the bedroom." Dickinson was faced with the choice of sounding the now hackneyed chants of the American Renaissance or reflecting upon the death of America's adolescent dream. "After thirty," Emerson had written in anticipation of the America the Amherst poet would have to celebrate, "a man wakes up sad every morning excepting perhaps five or six until the day of his death." By thirty-one Emily Dickinson knew all too well that cadaverous feeling:

> There's a certain Slant of light,
> Winter Afternoons –
> That oppresses, like the Heft
> Of Cathedral Tunes –
>
> Heavenly Hurt, it gives us –
> We can find no scar,
> But internal difference,
> Where the Meanings, are –
>
> None may teach it – Any –
> 'Tis the Seal Despair –
> An imperial affliction
> Sent us of the Air –
>
> When it comes, the Landscape listens –
> Shadows – hold their breath –
> When it goes, 'tis like the Distance
> On the look of Death –   (J. 258)

Having already experienced the ecstasy, America was well into its winter of discontent. And so we find no mystical experiences in the poet who was called back – again and again – to the hard facts of experience.

As late as 1855 the poet could proclaim, "I sound my barbaric yawp over the roofs of the world." By 1860 the American poet was forced to speak with a "Granite lip" (J. 182). Whitman reflects the change, of course, in such later poems as "Out of the Cradle Endlessly Rocking" and "As I Ebb'd with the Ocean of Life." Yet these tell of a loss of love and life. Dickinson's art, on the other hand, never takes the poet into battle; it never allows the actual to compromise the real:

To fight aloud, is very brave –
But *gallanter,* I know
Who charge within the bosom
The Cavalry of Wo –

Who win, and nations do not see –
Who fall – and none observe –
Whose dying eyes, no Country
Regards with patriot love –

We trust, in plumed procession
For such, the Angels go –
Rank after Rank, with even feet –
And Uniforms of Snow.   (J. 126)

Before *his* long silence, Melville had sought a "patriot love." But he soon realized, as he told his neighbor Hawthorne in 1851, that the teller of truth was usually sent packing to the "soup societies." Indeed, the paradox created by the demand for "popular art" (both then and today) serves up a metaphor for the aesthetic dilemma Dickinson confronted. The reading public (another oxymoron, perhaps) demands the actual – will not tolerate the real in its literature. It wishes to see only the body – the life with the HAPPY ENDING instead of the disembodied voice which signals THE END.

Dickinson knew better than Melville and so preferred not to publish. But neither did she retreat into the dead-letter office, as Melville symbolically does in his short story "Bartleby, The Scrivener." She wrote instead as the experienced virgin. This is an important distinction. Her work contains none of the "strong poetry" that propelled her literary predecessors into the spirit of the American Renaissance. We find no Ahabs writing their autobiographies "in colossal cipher." The "Cavalry of Wo" was enough for her, and indeed the only experience available to the poet on the eve of America's quarrel with itself. "The reason why the world lacks unity, and lies broken and in heaps," Emerson had written in *Nature,* "is, because man is disunited with himself." The war, however, reduced not only the hope of the actual but the scope of the real in America. Emerson's "slumbering giant" was now reduced to Dickinson's "supposed person." Now the actual and the real – like the atom in the modern era her poetry introduces – were split forever. The implication in Emerson's writing and those of the American Renaissance it inspired is that once man reconciles himself to the spirit, the body will follow. That is, life becomes as much a reality as death, and a poet of both body and soul is possible. But such a resurrection was not possible for Dickinson. Her "mind alone" never quite got past the crucifixion of the body.

"The dead sleep in their moonless night; my business is with the living," Emerson resolved in 1825. Of course, he went on to combine the life with the afterlife. For Dickinson, however, the dead were always dead –

> Safe in their Alabaster Chambers –
> Untouched by Morning
> And untouched by Noon –

The years, as noted earlier, go by without them. They are, in fact, the objects of time's mockery that measures their existence not even with the "peals of distant ironical laughter" Whitman heard at the end of the American Renaissance, but with soundless dots "on a Disc of Snow" (J. 216).

It was time, therefore, to try a new "language experiment." The marriage of the body and the soul had not worked out. America's literary renaissance, or "rebirth" as we like to forget, had been literally impossible. It had been an affront to nature itself since nothing ever comes *back* to life. There could be no New Eden; the old one would have to serve. This was Dickinson's realization at the beginning of the 1860s, as she came into her years of greatest productivity as a poet. The "slumbering giant" would have to be awakened again. And the meaning to which he awoke would be found not in the hopeful projection of the body into the soul but in the language that was essentially displaced from the body. Dickinson sensed what we now know as physiological fact: that language is not, strictly understood, a biological function. As one linguistic anthropologist writes, "Primary laryngeal patterns of behavior have had to be completely overhauled by the interferences of lingual, labial, and nasal modifications before a 'speech organ' was ready for work." Speech, then, is a physical activity that is somewhat beyond the body and perhaps a product of the "mind alone," since its use of physical organs does not correspond to the primary and original functions of the organs.

It was about this time that Dickinson began her retreat. Speech may have been beyond the body, but it was not, as she realized, beyond society, which always sought to scatter the original force of the writer. Rather than liberate the self from the body and its death sentence, *talking* drew the self back into society and the conversations there were ultimately pointless. There were talkers and there were writers. The first group faced one another endlessly; the second always sat face to face with themselves anew. The talker spoke almost exclusively of the body or society, whereas the writer retreated from the body politic and experi-

enced a "new wakefulness of words." The writer selected her own society and so became the "supposed person" – the one whose supposition
of a separate and eternal identity was possible only through language of
the "mind alone." Bathed in silent syllables of writing,

> The thought beneath so slight a film –
> Is more distinctly seen –
> As laces just reveal the surge –
> Or Mists – the Appenine –   (J. 210)

The self that emerged from such a "conversation" was not the product
of talk – that great soap that washes away more than the "film" that
separates the talker from the writer. If one desired to find out more about
his existence, he had to do more than *talk about it*. But doing more also
had its psychic costs. When one left the world of talk, the chart or script
was also abandoned. In the end the consequences of the artistic flight
were cruelly ironic, for one was always being called back to the world of
talk and the threat of THE END.

> What would the Dower be,
> Had I the Art to stun myself
> With Bolts of Melody!   (J. 505)

Emily Dickinson was about to find out.

Chapter 3

THE "HANSOM" MAN

In "Because I Could Not Stop for Death" (J. 712), Death is a most civil servant. He comes cordially and "kindly" stops for us. Yet his actual appearance is all the more shocking because the approach has been veiled with so much civility. Indeed, Death seduces the narrator of the poem with the beauty of nature. This was the paradox that Dickinson expressed at the height of her powers as a poet. To become, as Emerson had urged, in harmony with nature was to court her own destruction. The poet of Amherst, therefore, "could not stop for Death" in the way of Emerson and Whitman because she knew it would take her beyond the "mind alone" – or the limits of language itself. Words may have been signs of natural facts, but it did not necessarily follow that natural facts were (favorable) signs of spiritual facts. What indeed language suggested over and over was that words were our only protection – euphemisms in the face of certain annihilation. Language, it seemed, was the last outpost in a wilderness of natural facts.

The language of such a psychic settlement is most immediately suggested in the vernacular of jurisprudence, a science that Dickinson was acquainted with through her lawyer-father. Shortly before his conversion to Christianity in 1850, Edward Dickinson was told by his pastor, "You want to come to Christ as a *lawyer.*" The elder Dickinson required more proof that Christ was divine and the universe therefore an orderly place. Hearsay evidence or "faith" might have been a "fine intervention," but it would not serve in a court of law, that place where well-meaning people attempt to make sense of the irrational. Emily shared her father's desire for *"Microscopes,"* but she also realized that such a "legal" endeavor led to what Emerson called the corruption of language. That is, it called for language not simpler in its approach to paradox but a jargon that was labyrinthine in its attempt to understand and articulate the irrational. For truth, as Melville taught us in *Billy Budd,* has "ragged edges" that no court vernacular can ever trim. In fact, in that novel he

32

mocks the very attempt to make the lawyer's truth the poet's truth. Both Melville and Dickinson knew that to tell the truth, one had to tell it slant. And they both ridiculed attempts to tell it otherwise. In *Billy Budd* the "legal view" transforms nouns into verbs and relative clauses into funhouse mirrors, as we learn that "the apparent victim of the tragedy was he who had sought to victimize a man blameless; and the indisputable deed of the latter, navally regarded, constituted the most heinous of military crimes." Dickinson as effectively parodies the "legal view" in "Because I Could Not Stop for Death." The Emersonian (and Whitmanesque) idea of death as a transfer and promotion is no more palatable than the "navally regarded" idea of justice in *Billy Budd*. Instead of the absolute despondency that precedes the moment of death, we have the "hansom" man, the gentleman caller who "knew no haste." Instead of that final drowning of all physical sensation, we have the dying person's leisurely surrender to Death's "Civility." The death throe itself is parodied as a hansom ride toward eternity, its satire underscored by the sentimental references to schoolyard games and "Fields of Gazing Grain." With such imagery the speaker and her handsome man can pass even the "Setting Sun" – or almost.

It is at this point that the protective power of language recedes and the "harmony" of nature reveals itself as nothing more than a facade or "pasteboard mask" that finally tricks us out of life. The idea that a friendly order exists in nature is also ridiculed in "After Great Pain, a Formal Feeling Comes" (J. 341). The pain from loss is followed by the formality of "The stiff Heart," which is possible only through the illusions of language. We manage to outlive "the Hour of Lead" and try our luck again with the "harmony" of nature. We bury our grief (and the personal fear that accompanies it) in the pretensions about life's order. We return to the view that "It will be Summer – eventually" (J. 342):

> Ladies – with parasols –
> Sauntering Gentlemen – with Canes –
> And little Girls – with Dolls –
>
> Will tint the pallid landscape –
> As 'twere a bright Boquet –
> Tho' drifted deep, in Parian –
> The Village lies – today

As the snowy corpse of winter melts into summer, so does our grief give way to the seasons of life. Soothed by language, the melancholy *lets go*. Just as the promise of permanence in the particular is about to be dashed by nature's law of inevitable and relentless change, another promise of childhood and adolescence comes into view and the cycle of pastoral possibility begins anew. Despite the overwhelming grief over particular change, a time will come again when gentlemen saunter with canes, ladies twirl parasols, and little girls are forever "with Dolls."

It was language alone, and not words as signs of spiritual facts, that protected us from the terrible "harmony" of nature. It gave the "lie" that told the truth of the "mind alone." Somewhere between body and soul we existed. With our words we pronounced ourselves fit subjects for the contemplation that evidenced our existence. Considering the human dilemma, it was a "white" lie but one whose color was as inscrutable as God Himself. Dickinson lied to stay alive and indeed began her semi-public career as a poet with a lie when she told Higginson she had "made no verse – but one or two – until this winter." This was indirectly in answer to how old *she* was, but her lie told the same truth Melville's did when he told Hawthorne he had experienced no intellectual growth until the age of twenty-five. In each case the poet announced his intellectual catharsis – or "birthday." Melville was well on his way to completing his masterpiece in *Moby-Dick,* and Dickinson was already at her zenith as one of America's greatest poets. Indeed, today her vision seems as stark as Melville's.

This "lie" to Higginson is surely the poet's literary declaration of independence, her "letter to the World" she knew would never write back to her. As such it takes its place with Melville's bold statements about himself to Hawthorne and Whitman's open letter to Emerson. Melville lied to Hawthorne and Whitman lied to Emerson because in both cases the liars found their autobiographies "writ large" in the work of their correspondents. In lying to Higginson, however, Dickinson was really lying to herself on the second story. That is to say, she had first as a female poet no reliable literary models; second, as a poet her life of the "mind alone" corresponded to no biography whatever. Hers was the poetry of the second self or mind that always found itself without its "corporeal friend."

Higginson, of course, was in no way prepared for the experimental poetry this world view produced, and we must give him credit for not dismissing Dickinson out of hand as slightly mad. A veteran at advising lady poets, he doubtless hoped (in responding to the first batch of poems sent) that he was dealing with another Helen Hunt Jackson, Harriet Prescott Spofford, or Rose Terry. But to his suggestion that she state her ideas in the literary convention of the day, Dickinson merely thanked him for the "surgery" and protested, "While my thought is undressed – I can make the distinction, but when I put them in the Gown – they look alike and numb." It was the difference between the thoughts of the poetaster and those of a poet. Conventional thought, like conventional verse, was just *that* – "alike and numb" in its courtship of the sentimental. It was the language of legality, words properly dressed for nature's slaughter. Dickinson's language, on the other hand, threw off convention and risked everything.

Higginson's letter to Dickinson is lost, but we know from her answer to it that he recommended that she consider the work of Harriet Prescott Spofford (1835–1921) as her model. There is no evidence Dickinson thought much of Spofford's poetry or even that she had read it, but we do know that she was much taken by the writer's short fiction, which had been appearing regularly in the *Atlantic Monthly* since February 1859. "I read Miss Prescott's 'Circumstance,' " she told Higginson, "but it followed me, in the Dark – so I avoided her." Written in the mode of a captivity narrative, the story appeared in the *Atlantic* of May 1860. Its bizarre but sentimental plot sheds light on Dickinson's state of mind as she both wrote to Higginson and composed her finest poems. It reads like a dream-vision, indeed a nightmare. And as with most captivity narratives, it is both violent and sensual. The story concerns a Maine woman who while returning at dusk from a neighbor's farm is seized by an "Indian Devil," a creature half animal, half human. "His long sharp claws were caught in her clothing, he worried them sagaciously a little, then finding that ineffectual to free them, he commenced licking her bare white arm with his rasping tongue and pouring over her the wide streams of his hot, fetid breath." At first the woman cries out for her husband (who does arrive to kill the beast but not until she has endured a night of terror). She soon discovers, however, that the beast, who has already rendered her arm "once white, now crimson," can be calmed by her singing. The rest of the narrative is occupied with the sadomasochistic description of her ordeal as she strains her voice to save her life. Whenever it failed her, "the long red tongue [of the monster] was thrust forth again. Before it touched, a song sprang from her lips."

To sing was to fill the darkness with words. "You wonder why I write – so," she told her friend Mary Bowles that spring. "Because I cannot help." Almost a year later, as already noted, she told her cousins, "Let Emily sing for you because she cannot pray." The woman in the story cannot pray either, cannot project herself into a safer future: "She did not think at this instant to call upon God. She called upon her husband." But the calls are useless until they metamorphose into song: "Just this point between life and death intensified every faculty – and when she opened her lips the third time, it was not for shrieking, but for singing." The terror abates only when words are employed as words and not as conveyances back to the "harmony" of nature. Out of those intense moments of ratio between life and death came the song of the "mind alone" in the present. For Dickinson at the height of her poetic powers, these moments were almost routine: "I had a terror – since September – I could tell to none – and so I sing, as the Boy does by the Burying Ground – because I am afraid."

This was Dickinson's captivity narrative. In his "Letter to a Young Contributor," Higginson had spoken of poetry as a "decent *clothing of words.*" Yet there was nothing "decent" about the poet whose language was stripped by the savagery of nature of any assurances about the future. Nothing was left the poet – no cordiality, no "clothing of words." She sang as the Indian did by the grave of his loved one because the truth of the present, as she also told Higginson in a poem, came to her "Bald, and Cold" (J. 281). Stripped of the illusions that characterized the writings of her contemporaries, her words measured the possibility not of a vague future but of a present in which the ratio between life and death was the only reality.

Students of Dickinson have remarked on the poet's relatively few (extant) allusions to the war that was raging as she wrote her best poetry. The war and the poetry, however, were not mutually exclusive. Dickinson was shocked by the carnage – jolted in fact into a mental disturbance that produced in 1862 more poems, and better poems, than in any other period of the artist's life. Her letter of December 31, 1861, to Louise Norcross is ample if almost solitary evidence of the way the war magnified the peacetime struggle between loving and living:

> Mrs. Adams had news of the death of her boy to-day, from a wound at Annapolis. Telegram signed by Frazer [*sic*] Stearns. You remember him. Another died in October – from fever caught in the camp. Mrs. Adams herself has not risen from bed since then. "Happy new year" step softly over such doors as these! "Dead! Both her boys! One of them shot by the sea in the East, and one of them shot in the West by the sea." . . . Christ be merciful! Frazer Stearns is just leaving Annapolis. His father has gone to see him to-day. I hope that ruddy face won't be brought home frozen.

Not more than a month before Dickinson confessed to Higginson that she sang "as the Boy does by the Burying Ground" Lieutenant Stearns, the son of the president of Amherst College, was killed at the Battle of Newbern.

After the same North Carolina battle, the brother of Walt Whitman told his mother: "We have given the Secesshers another thundering thrashing, and have gained a splendid victory." George Washington Whitman added, "I went through the fight and did not get a scratch although the balls fairly rained around me, and several of our boys were struck down close by my side." Unlike his poet-brother, who knew that the actual horror of the war "will never be written – perhaps must not and should not be," George went through the conflict with few scratches, emotional or otherwise. Somehow Walt Whitman of New York and Emily Dickinson of Massachusetts knew the war better than the soldiers who fought it. Whitman's observations in *Specimen Days* (1882) show it. Dickinson's comments to her cousin about Mrs. Adams's boys show it. They both experienced its unreasonable wound. Frazar Stearns's "big heart," Emily added, was "shot away by a 'minie ball.' "

In this sense, she knew the war better than Higginson, who had led the first black regiment into combat and who had been wounded in action. This was her message in her letters to him. To the poet for whom "the noise in the Pool, at Noon – excels my Piano," the sound of gunfire was deafening. Her letter of April 25, 1862, for example, is fraught with the pathos that is merely exaggerated in war: She had been ill and writes from her "pillow"; she had a terror since September; she "had a friend, who taught me Immortality – but venturing too near himself – he never returned"; she found another tutor, "but he was not contented I be his scholar – and so left the Land." She asks Higginson how to "grow," yet answers her own question by saying that it is "unconveyed – like Melody," or immortality. Growth was "harmony" with nature, and what an irresistible growth it was now – so speeded up by war. It was the race from mortality to "immortality," and the only way to *convey* this paradox was to sing about it. There was no other way to understand it, no other way to keep the "Indian Devil" at bay. When Frazar Stearns died, Emily saw the irony about *particular* growth. Higginson, on the other hand, never took his eyes off the general life that survived the war. In the preface to a biographical memoir to Harvard boys killed in the war, he wrote, "I do not see how any one can read these memoirs without being left with fresh confidence in our institutions, in the American people, and indeed in human nature itself." This was terror with a happy ending.

For Higginson particular death was always dressed in a "decent *clothing of words*":

> We slowly drove – He knew no haste
> And I had put away
> My labor and my leisure too,
> For His Civility –   (J. 712)

Dickinson might have said with Whitman, "I see through the broadcloth and gingham whether or no," but Higginson was prepared only to hear that the poet who saw the war the way Emily did was "disgraceful." He was prepared not for the "naked truth" but for truth decked out in "fresh confidence." And so he missed much, if not all, of her message – in the letter of April 25 as well as in the three poems she enclosed with it.

In the first of these, the sound of war contrasts sharply with the sounds she hears:

> Of all the Sounds despatched abroad,
> There's not a Charge to me
> Like that old measure in the Boughs –
> That phraseless Melody –
> The Wind does – working like a Hand
> Whose fingers Comb the Sky –
> Then quiver down – with tufts of Tune –
> Permitted God, and me –

Like "the noise in the Pool," the wind is a "phraseless," or *unconveyed,* melody. Later in the poem she calls it "that fleshless Chant." No wonder this poet has been accused of ignoring the Civil War – when she can write about the wind instead of the "winds of war." But the battle imagery is in fact what makes this poem work. Phrases like "Sounds despatched abroad" and "a Charge to Me" remind us of the more famous "Success Is Counted Sweetest" (J. 67). Also, the chant after a bloody battle is almost as fleshless as the wind – often the only sound:

> I crave Him grace of Summer Boughs,
> If such an Outcast be –
> Who never heard that fleshless Chant –
> Rise – solemn – on the Tree,
> As if some Caravan of Sound
> Off Deserts, in the Sky,
> Had parted Rank,
> Then knit, and swept –
> In Seamless Company –   (J. 321)

The wind is perhaps the sound of "the parted Rank" – the dying soldier of life who returns to the ranks of God "In Seamless Company." If such a reading sounds simplistic and melodramatic, it is because lines 9–24 of the poem have not been quoted or yet considered. Without them we get a clearer, more coherent definition of the wind and its effect on the poet. Higginson liked clear-definition poems, and his preference shows in the 1890 edition, where we encounter the categories of "Life," "Love," "Nature," and "Time and Eternity." It also shows in the September 1890 issue of the *Christian Union,* where he published the poem without the lines in question. Higginson wanted something left after the truth about the present was told: He wanted the slaughter to produce "fresh confidence in our institutions, in the American people, and indeed in human nature itself." But Dickinson knew that the truth always left us with the kind of uneasy ambiguity described in lines 9–24:

Inheritance, it is, to us –
Beyond the Art to Earn –
Beyond the trait to take away
By Robber, since the Gain
Is gotten not of fingers –
And inner than the Bone –
Hid golden, for the whole of Days,
And even in the Urn,
I cannot vouch the merry Dust
Do not arise and play
In some odd fashion of it's own.
Some quainter Holiday,
When Winds go round and round in Bands –
And thrum upon the door,
And Birds take places, overhead,
To bear them Orchestra.

In the 1890 edition of her *Poems* these lines are also missing. The poem is entitled "The Wind," of course, and it is found in the "Nature" category. The whole poem, however, is not so easily classified, for it is also about "Life," "Love," "Nature," and "Time and Eternity" (Higginson's euphemism for "Death"). Like every great poem, it has all these themes bound up not by easy assumptions but by an odd satisfaction in the failure of the promises of childhood and adolescence. The "Gain," we are told, "Is gotten not of fingers" but is "inner than the Bone." Even in "the Urn" our remains remain "In some odd fashion of [their] own."

Higginson saw only what he wanted to see in Dickinson's poetry, but the fact is that he did see somehow her "odd" genius. By the late 1880s, when he and Mabel Todd were preparing a selection of the poems for Roberts Brothers, he at least knew how to edit Dickinson to his own expectations. The second poem she sent with her letter of April 25 also found its way into the first edition as "Renunciation." The strongest of the three she sent, its subject, as one critic has suggested, has as much to do with commitment as with giving up:

There came a Day at Summer's full,
Entirely for me –
I thought that such were for the Saints,
Where Resurrections – be –

The Sun, as common, went abroad,
The flowers, accustomed, blew,

As if no soul the solstice passed
That maketh all things new –

The time was scarce profaned, by speech –
The symbol of a word
Was needless, as at Sacrament,
The Wardrobe – of our Lord –

Each was to each The Sealed Church,
Permitted to commune this – time –
Lest we too awkward show
At Supper of the Lamb.

The Hours slid fast – as Hours will,
Clutched tight, by greedy hands –
So faces on two Decks, look back,
Bound to opposing lands –

And so when all the time had leaked,
Without external sound
Each bound the Other's Crucifix –
We gave no other Bond –

Sufficient troth, that we shall rise –
Deposed – at length, the Grave –
To that new Marriage,
Justified – through Calvaries of Love –   (J. 322)

Variously read as a love poem about parting, a poem of religious dedication, or one describing a mystical or real marriage, the poem both
invites and eludes interpretation. But if we consider it as part of Emily's
letter to Higginson and as such part of her literary manifesto, a new
reading emerges. The poem is really about language at the limits of civility – "at Summer's full" (or "fall") and the arrival of the "hansom"
man. In fact, both the theme and structure are remarkably similar to
those of "Because I Could Not Stop for Death." In each poem the visitor
arrives and the language of civility fails. In J. 322 the "symbol of a word"
becomes as useless "as at Sacrament, / The Wardrobe – of our Lord."
That is, the "decent *clothing of words*" no longer hides the naked truth that
"salvation" requires the ultimate sacrifice. In J. 712 the poet's illusion
that death will never come ("We passed the Setting Sun") also proves
inadequate:

The Dews drew quivering and chill –
For only Gossamer, my Gown –
My Tippet – only Tulle –

In J. 322 the speaker at "Summer's full" is exhilarated by the same illusion about nature:

> The Sun, as common, went abroad,
> The flowers, accustomed, blew,
> As if no soul the solstice passed
> That maketh all things new

The truth is, however, that the sun sets upon our lives, and its solstice at "Summer's full" (the June 22nd of our lives) will pass to make "all things new." As in J. 712 we have here a dying and a resurrection – a catharsis of language and the birth of a poet. One life (or language) is renounced for another. In a sense, both poems announce the "Second Coming" of language: "Justified – through Calvaries of Love." Like Whitman's "Out of the Cradle Endlessly Rocking," these poems chronicle the poet's discovery of her vocation. Hers is the language not of "Time and Eternity" but of love and death. As such it embraces the awful paradox that Higginson's language merely sentimentalizes.

The third poem enclosed with her letter was doubtless more to Higginson's liking. It was appropriately entitled "With Flowers" in the second book of *Poems* (1891), as it was written to accompany flowers. Perhaps intended as a greeting to Higginson, it also stood in sharp contrast to the two other poems she sent. Those echoed Poe's lament about time in "Israfel" that "Our flowers are merely – flowers." This one simply presented the flowers and asked no disturbing questions:

> South Winds jostle them –
> Bumblebees come –
> Hover – Hesitate – Drink, and are gone –
> Butterflies pause – on their passage Cashmere –
> I, softly plucking,
> Present them – Here –   (J.86)

But the flowers really belonged to Dickinson, as she greeted herself at the beginning of a great career. As we have remarked, Higginson was no Whitman's Emerson. About the time he had probably already received Dickinson's first four poems (sent in her initial letter to him), he complained to his editor, James T. Fields, "I foresee that 'Young Contributors' will send me worse things than ever now. Two such specimens of verse as came yesterday & day before – fortunately *not* to be forwarded for publication!" At best what he got in response to his *Atlantic* article were "wonderful effusions." But Dickinson knew what she was about. She told Mrs. Holland, the wife of another literary arbiter, "Perhaps the whole United States are laughing at me. . . . *I* can't stop for that ! *My* business is to love."

It would be another eight years before Higginson would get around to visiting the person behind the letters and poems he had been receiving from Amherst. In the meantime Dickinson was content to be one of his "scholars" but as such "the only Kangaroo among the Beauty." It is clearer than some critics would like to admit that Dickinson was serious when she told Higginson in her third letter that publication was as foreign to her "as Firmament to Fin." She wrote, as she told him, to relieve the "palsy." Dollars could not damn *her* the way they did Melville. What she felt most moved to write may have been "banned" by the Higginsons and the Hollands of the world, but like Whitman, who reviewed his own work anonymously, Dickinson was essentially satisfied with her audience of one. There was also, of course, the outlet of relatives and friends through letters. Higginson, it might be said, was finally no more than another correspondent.

It is also probably no coincidence that she took up her correspondence with Higginson when another "mentor," Samuel Bowles, went abroad. Although we might hesitate to accept the thesis that Bowles was the poet's "master," we do know that she counted on having the editor of the *Springfield Republican* as part of her audience. In fact, Dickinson thrived on having, besides herself, an audience of her own selection ("her own Society") – every writer's impossible dream but hers, it appears. With Bowles more or less out of reach, she turned to Higginson to fill his place. What is noteworthy about the substitution is that for the first time she went outside her circle of family and friends. Bowles was a friend of the family. Sue Dickinson became part of the family. The others earned their right to read her through either sibling or adolescent relationships. And yet out of the blue, on April 15, 1862, she asked a stranger "to say if my Verse is alive?"

Even more interesting is the fact that she was drawn out of her retreat by a "Letter to a Young Contributor." Dickinson was already thirty-one years of age, not exactly young in the nineteenth century. Indeed, she has hardly more than another twenty years to live. Recently, it has been observed that Dickinson acted out the role of the rebellious daughter at a time when her contemporaries were grandmothers. This was her persona, the argument goes, to her father and all men, including those in the literary establishment such as Higginson. But the "act" – if it was one – was more than a literary facade. Dickinson herself was both genuinely shy and intellectually rebellious. Evidence of that combination is most readily found in Higginson's record of his first interview with the poet, when she was almost forty years old.

By preserving what must be considered one of the most remarkable scenes in American literary history (only Melville's last meeting with

Hawthorne in Liverpool in 1856 and Whitman's encounter with Emerson on Boston Common in 1860 are comparable), Higginson more than compensated for the injury he tried to do Whitman's reputation. We can even forgive him for failing to mention Dickinson in his memoir, *Cheerful Yesterdays* (1898). Apparently, when the former clergyman met the poet in Amherst, he was shocked out of the Victorian paternalism he reserved for women and blacks. As he told his wife after the initial meeting on August 16, 1870, "I was never with any one who drained my nerve power so much. Without touching her, she drew from me." He added readily, "I am glad not to live near her."

Curiously, this impression contrasts dramatically with the description of her person and demeanor as she first entered the room. Higginson recalled that Dickinson approached him with the "step like a pattering child's." "She came to me," he told his wife, "with two day lilies which she put in a sort of childlike way into my hand & said 'These are my introduction' in a soft frightened breathless childlike voice." Like the flowers she had vicariously sent him eight years earlier with "South Winds Jostle Them" (J. 86), flowers were indeed her introduction. In retrospect we might view them as mocking the civility that precedes the truth. Higginson remembered that the poet "added under her breath Forgive me if I am frightened; I never see strangers & hardly know what to say – but she talked soon & thenceforward continuously – & deferentially – sometimes stopping to ask me to talk instead of her – but readily recommencing." Suddenly Higginson found this "little girl" who never saw strangers holding forth on matters both profound and paradoxical. Showing the confidence of a Thoreau before his "John or Jonathan," she proceeded to "dazzle" him with her particular "slant" on the truth. This is a rare moment in the Dickinson biography, one of the few in which the disembodied voice – like the nineteenth-century "table-rappers" the believers in spiritualism sought – inhabits something less "fleshless" than a chant. But Higginson was no more prepared for the "corporeal friend" than he had been for the "mind alone." Twenty-one years later he recalled his hope of bringing their relationship "down to the level of simple truth and every-day comradeship."

Simple truth and everyday comradeship are, of course, the subjects of poetasters and not poets. They were the playthings of all those lady poets who got published in the *Atlantic Monthly*. "Perhaps you smile at me," she suggested back in 1862 in her fourth letter to Higginson. "I could not stop for that – My Business is Circumference." Her poetry went full circle with the truth. It made "Yesterday mean" – dead time on our hands. The full statement is "Today, makes Yesterday mean." The truth was always now, in the immediate present. It was not, however, the transcendentalist's present. That enclosed the past and the future. Dickinson's present negated them both. This poet distilled

> . . . amazing sense
> From ordinary Meanings –
> And Attar so immense
> From the familiar species
> That perished by the Door   (J. 448)

This poet was, with the exception of the timeless present, "Exterior to time." She left the illusions of "simple truth and every-day comradeship" to the lawyers and literati of her day.

Another poem written in 1862 makes this Dickinsonian distinction even sharper:

> I died for Beauty – but was scarce
> Adjusted in the Tomb
> When One who died for Truth, was lain
> In an adjoining Room –
>
> He questioned softly "Why I failed"?
> "For Beauty", I replied –
> "And I – for Truth – Themself are One –
> We Bretheren, are", He said –
>
> And so, as Kinsmen, met a Night –
> We talked between the Rooms –
> Until the Moss had reached our lips –
> And covered up – our names –   (J. 449)

Higginson (and Mrs. Todd) called the poem "Two Kinsmen" in the 1890 edition. But in finding truth and beauty synonymous, they were probably not echoing Keats's (or Dickinson's) view of these two concepts. Truth and beauty combined, as Keats wrote, to form a "Cold Pastoral." The one is forever contradicting the other. They are always together – and never:

> Beauty is truth, truth beauty, – that is all
> Ye know on earth, and all ye need to know

Truth and beauty were "Kinsmen" in the way Madeline and Roderick are in Poe's "The Fall of the House of Usher." The one (truth) caused the death of the other (beauty). One was general, the other particular. And when they met, time passed. "But I was going to say when Truth broke in," Robert Frost wrote in "Birches." The truth was always breaking in on the promises – or in Frost's poem, the memories – of childhood and adolescence.

Beauty was always being ravished by the truth. It was better therefore to remain in the exclusive present. Here the poet distilled amazing sense from the "familiar species / That perished by the Door." Beauty survived only in the environment of constant abstinence, as Dickinson concluded in another poem written about 1862, "I Cannot Live with You";

> So We must meet apart –
> You there – I – here –
> With just the Door ajar
> That Oceans are – and Prayer –
> And that White Sustenance –
> Despair –   (J. 640)

Abstinence was sustenance – "White Sustenance." It was that inscrutable quality of life. The "Door ajar" might as well be the expanse "That Oceans are." Yet the hound, bay horse, and turtle dove that Thoreau sought in *Walden* could not be so safely in the distance; they had always to be just out of sight.

It is in the context of this paradox about beauty and truth that we must reexamine the famous and puzzling "My Life Had Stood – a Loaded Gun" (J. 754). The pluperfect tense in the opening line makes this another "posthumous" poem, in the way of "Because I Could Not Stop for Death" (J. 712). The problem, however, lies in determining the identity of the speaker. In J. 712 it is the "supposed person" who has died. In J. 754 it is something that cannot die – namely, a gun. To put the matter in broader terms, the speaker has power, but it is firepower instead of willpower. As Edwards argues in *Freedom of Will* (c. 1754), man is relatively helpless in the sense that he cannot *will* his will but only act it out. In the poem, only the "Owner" can pull the trigger. As the "inanimate" narrator confesses:

> My Life had stood – a Loaded Gun
> In Corners – till a Day
> The Owner passed – identified –
> And carried Me away

Later in the poem we are frustrated to learn not only that the helpless narrator "may longer live" than the "Owner" or God but that the narrator – or man – has

> . . . but the power to kill,
> Without – the power to die –

It will not do to dismiss, as critics have lately, Dickinson's most difficult poems by observing that they go off into the silence of an "unanchored tropism." Going there is in fact her relentless theme, but none of her poems ever gets there. Ever and anon they stop with the conflict between beauty and truth. And the *truth* in "My Life Had Stood – a Loaded Gun" is that man may "outlive" God in the sense that God's creation or will is eternal (indeed, so omnipotent that it can create the unliftable rock). Hence, a man will go on infinitely in the mind of God, but – and this is Dickinson's tragic concern in the poem – not in the particular. There he is in no way infinite but *very* indefinite.

He is indefinite because he lacks "the power to die" or the ability to change on his own. Rather, he is a victim of the cosmic will because all he can do is shoot or "kill" when fired. And yet man and God are no more adversaries than the "master" and his gun. For the "Owner" pulls the trigger and thus allows the *beauty* of the particular life to flourish, however instantaneously on the "range" of eternity. With the final shot our beauty explodes into the truth of the general life. Dickinson is not so much concerned with what happens at that moment, only with the thought of it – or death – which animates the real "talk" of life until, as she writes in "I Died for Beauty," the "Moss" reaches our lips and covers "up – our names." We died, in fact, for both beauty and truth because, like the power to kill and the power to die, they are ultimately the same thing. Beauty *is* change, and so when man is ultimately killed, he dies. This is the view of the posthumous, inanimate narrator, but the concern of the present narrator – the writer Dickinson – is the beauty of life itself in the present. What is beautiful about life in the present is that beauty and truth are always together and never because life is death – or change – only in *process*. And it is this truth of the Not-Me that becomes more important to us than any ultimate truth in the mind of God or Real Me. The particular life is more important than the general or universal life because in the latter all we have is the fired gun and the truth that our potential as "corporeal friend[s]" is exhausted. We strive, therefore, to remain the "Loaded Gun" always before our "Cold Pastoral." We remain silently loaded with language that will someday "convict" us of the capital offense of existing in the first place.

In Dickinson's world view, the particular life is everything and nothing – the first and last illusion. The particular is full of words, and the general is grim with silence. "Vesuvius dont talk – Etna – dont," we will recall from the second "Master" letter (and by this juncture there should be less doubt about who the "master" in those letters ultimately is). "One of them – said a syllable – a thousand years ago, and Pompeii heard it, and hid forever." This naming power of the volcano of truth that language finally uncovers is also a maiming power. In *Nature* and elsewhere Emerson observes that nature could have ministered to our basic needs without being beautiful. To the transcendentalist, this is evidence of a meaningful existence in the particular. But to the determinist of Amherst, beauty is its own excuse for being. Life was always beautiful *until* it was condemned to the truth of the universal:

And do I smile, such cordial light
Upon the Valley glow –
It is as a Vesuvian face
Had let it's pleasure through –   (J. 754)

The Vesuvian face of truth is always burying the Pompeii of beauty.
Once beauty is targeted or "identified" (J. 754), it assumes "the power
to die." The power of language, therefore, is the loaded gun without a
target, for once its sights are set, beauty is finished.

Or once the lover comes, the ecstasy is finished. This is the theme of
"Because I Could Not Stop for Death," the companion piece, surely, of
J. 754. The "hansom" man stops by; he and the narrator make love in a
"House" that becomes "A Swelling of the Ground." It is important to
remember in reading this poem that the carriage holds not only the
gentleman caller and the speaker but also "Immortality." The reunion
(for life is memory in Dickinson's world) begins slowly ("He knew no
haste"), but before she knows it the "Dews" are enough to chill her.
This is a negative version of Whitman's "procreant urge," for death is
emphasized instead of life. In both cases "Immortality" is celebrated, but
Dickinson's sense of it is merely that posthumous state (in the present
and not in the future) in which she can distance herself not only from the
fear of death but also from the language of civility that covers up that
fear by sentimentalizing it. Indeed, Dickinson's narrator scorns the happy
endings of the hymns and other popular forms of writing held up to
the poet by the Higginsons of the world as literary models. The speaker
is "saved" not from death but from the life that would endeavor to ig-
nore death. As a consequence she can now *remember* from the eternity of
the present:

                Since then – 'tis Centuries – and yet
                Feels shorter than the Day
                I first surmised the Horses Heads
                Were toward Eternity –   (J. 712)

This poem is about the day in every life when we realize that the desire
for love is the desire for death. All we have finally, Dickinson knew, is
the desire to love. And our lover does finally and kindly stop for us. We
seek to love ourselves into immortality. The poem describes the speaker's assignation with the lover she had always remembered. "For His
Civility," she waits in her gown of gossamer (not exactly the uniform
for a harmless carriage ride in public). Since the lover is death, the scene
is ultimately autoerotic. The speaker has exhausted all illusions about the
future and now seeks out the self in the present sense of the past.

"This one fact the world hates." Emerson had written in "Self-Reliance," "that the soul *becomes.*" As spokesman for American romanticism, Emerson saw wholeness as possible after rather than before the present. If man knew the direction of the "Horses Heads," he could live self-reliantly. In Dickinson's ontology, however, man is already posthumous to the time when he was whole. Whereas Emerson anticipates, Dickinson remembers. And what she recalls is the time when her lover was always coming but had yet to arrive. For once he does, sex in the subjunctive becomes sex in the imperative. The illusions of civility are dashed, and the "Soul" has ever afterward only "her own Society" to select.

All this is to say that Dickinson's future lay in the past. The life would always be the life that was – when indeed it consisted of those illusions. Life could not be lived, as Higginson and his lady poets imagined, in the future. Desiring "terror with a happy ending," they sought out a nature that mothered life instead of smothering it with autoerotic caresses. Rather than see death as Dickinson's "hansom" man, they preferred Longfellow's sexless version in his poem on "Nature." There death is perceived

> As a fond mother, [who] when the day is o'er,
> Leads by the hand her little child to bed.

At its best (as it surely is in J. 712) Dickinson's poetry mocks this kind of civility with its posthumous narrator, who looks back upon our hopes for a better future with a "metallic grin" that threatens to freeze the face of time.

Chapter 4

FATHER EMERSON
AND EMILY

In "A Wedding on Cape Rosier" the poet Richard Eberhart includes the lines

> Father Emerson puts out the candles
> His father knew Emily Dickinson

The poem describes an actual wedding in "a forest chapel" on the summery coast of Maine. Father Emerson, the chapel's owner and preacher, is also someone personally known to Eberhart. Indeed, in one sense Father Emerson was also known to Emily Dickinson, for the father of this man was one of the Amherst children who had regular access to the reclusive poet. In fact, Kendall Emerson became the surrogate for young Gilbert Dickinson, who as we may remember died at the age of eight in 1883. Apparently, the Emerson boy had played in the same mud hole where Gilbert contracted the typhoid fever from which he died. At Christmas time, only a couple of months after Gilbert's sudden death, the poet wrote to him, "Christmas in Bethlehem means most of all, this Year, but Santa Claus still asks the way to Gilbert's little friends – Is Heaven an unfamiliar road?" A year after Gilbert's death she told Sue Dickinson, in an oblique reference to Kendall Emerson, "Twice, when I had Red Flowers out, Gilbert knocked, raised his sweet Hat, and asked if he might touch them. Yes, and take them too, I said, but Chivalry forbade him – Besides, he gathered Hearts, not flowers."

In two other notes to the boy, penned on succeeding Christmases, she reminded him of the role she had assigned him. "Missing my own Boy, I knock at other Trundle-Beds, and trust the Curls are in." With her last extant note to him she enclosed a blossom and hoped he would not venture too deeply into the woods to play. By this time Dickinson was recovering from what her physician described as "Nervous prostration." But really she never got over the shock of young Gilbert's meteoric passage through her life. His disappearance seemed to coincide with the deaths of so many others – Charles Wadsworth, Samuel Bowles. "The Missing All," as she wrote in J. 985, may have prevented her from "missing minor Things," such as the end of the world ("a World's / Departure from a Hinge / Or Sun's extinction"), but conversely the threat of no existence could not overwhelm the very problem of existence itself. That existence consisted of absences that constantly needed filling. We yearned to connect with ourselves in what Whitman called the "huge first Nothing," but love was linear and time was circular. Locked into the present, the only way we could reach back to our original identity before the Fall was through surrogates.

By 1883, however, Emily Dickinson was down to her last surrogate in life. As one of her biographers remarks, "No death during E[mily] D[ickinson]'s lifetime more deeply shocked and grieved her." The "hansom" man had simply visited too often, and Kendall Emerson was her last chance: And had the child been a true surrogate or "lover" instead of simply a substitute for Gilbert, the poet might have been pulled out of her final slough in life. "If recollecting were forgetting," she had early announced to herself, "How near I had forgot." We were, as she knew, defined by what we once had been. In our subconscious quest for survival – and identity – we were always reestablishing through our lovers what Emerson has called in another context our "original relation to the universe."

The following poem suggests that the love of our lives is most deeply felt through the prism of memory:

> I see thee better – in the Dark –
> I do not need a Light –
> The Love of Thee – a Prism be –
> Excelling Violet –
>
> I see thee better for the Years
> That hunch themselves between –
> The Miner's Lamp – sufficient be –
> To nullify the Mine –
>
> And in the Grave – I see Thee best –
> It's little Panels be
> Aglow – All ruddy – with the Light
> I held so high, for Thee –
>
> What need of Day –
> To Those whose Dark – hath so – surpassing Sun –
> It deem it be – Continually –
> At the Meridian?
>
> (J. 611)

Though this poem can be read as an apostrophe to a lost lover, its meaning deepens when we see that apostrophe as an expression of self-love. In other words, the darker side of ourselves is illuminated by our love for others, who in turn keep us at the meridian of memory. Love is a kind of dying that brings us closer to our source:

> You'll find – it when you try to die –
> The Easier to let go –
> For recollecting such as went –
> You could not spare – you know.
>
> And though their places somewhat filled –
> As did their Marble names
> With Moss – they never grew so full –
> You chose the newer names –
>
> And when this World – sets farther back
> As Dying – say it does –
> The former lover – distincter grows –
> And supersedes the fresh –
>
> And Thought of them – so fair invites –
> It looks too tawdry Grace
> To stay behind – with just the Toys
> We bought – to ease their place –   (J. 610)

As Charles R. Anderson reminds us, poetry for Dickinson was "A fairer House than Prose" because it offered the freedom "for flights outward and upward." But the way outward was also the way inward, and so poetry relieved the prosaic moments of the present. It poeticized them by discovering the past in surrogates. It took one to the heart of experience, for surrogates were the very artifacts of experience. They were the next best thing to that which was forever elusive. This is not to say, of course, that Dickinson literally lived in the past. Probably no one else better recognized, as she told Higginson, the "ecstasy in living." She usually found the ecstasy, however, in her poetry, which allowed for the fusion of present and the past. There – in the subjunctive instead of the imperative – it was possible to have the ecstasy without the agony:

> I dwell in Possibility –
> A fairer House than Prose –
> More numerous of Windows –
> Superior – for Doors –

More will be said for the significance of windows (and not doors) in Dickinson's poetry. For now it is sufficient to observe that windows let in love without death, for poetry was, as she continues in the poem, a house of surrogates for that one first love:

> Of Visiters – the fairest –
> For Occupation – This –
> The spreading wide my narrow Hands
> To gather Paradise –   (J. 657)

Poetry was the house of "Possibility" in which the lonely crowd of the present were given back their identities in the ever-present past. It relieved the "palsy" of the present, what Dickinson called man's crippling preoccupation with "this brief Tragedy of Flesh" (J. 664).

That tragedy became clear as the promises of childhood and adolescence began to dissipate. Probably the most important of the poet's surrogates was Susan Dickinson, Austin's wife. As noted earlier, Sue was Emily's way of remaining the experienced virgin, that individual who could retain the freedom of adolescence in adulthood – or sex in the subjunctive. Therefore, when their tight relationship began to wane in 1861, when the birth of Ned Dickinson absorbed Sue's attention, Emily began to view the human dilemma with considerably more insight. It is not unreasonable to read "A Wife – at Daybreak" (J. 461), written about the time of Ned's birth and sent over the hedge to her sister-in-law, as the poet's realization that Sue was no longer willing to serve as a surrogate for conjugal and carnal experience. At best now, Sue was what Emily would soon call her "pseudo Sister," and Emily herself became the bride of experience:

> A Wife – at Daybreak I shall be –
> Sunrise – Hast thou a Flag for me?
> At Midnight, I am but a Maid,
> How short it takes to make it Bride –

She concludes the poem by announcing:

> I fumble at my Childhood's prayer
> So soon to be a Child no more –
> Eternity, I'm coming – Sir,
> Savior – I've seen the face – before!

Without Sue she was left to the pleasure of *"boots, and whiskers"* – to be ravished now, not in the second story of art, but in the life that had to be lived in the present. Christ, the archetype of carnal lovers – indeed, the "hansom" man of conventional religion – was no longer the harmless companion of fishermen, "Of freckled Human Nature" (J. 401). With Sue's transformation into the soft, cherubic creature of motherhood, Emily felt the full weight of experience. This, and not Wadsworth's departure for California in 1862, may have been the catalyst for her emotional instability. Her latest and ablest biographer remarks that Dickinson's relationship with Sue was one of the controlling influences of her life. Years later, when Austin had begun his affair with Mabel Loomis Todd, she confessed that with the exception of Shakespeare, Sue had "told [her] of more knowledge than any one living." The admission reminds us slightly of Melville's favorable comparison of Hawthorne and Shakespeare. In both cases the praise conjures up the "Prince of Poets" – in terms of influence, the writer's writer.

Who was Susan Dickinson, anyway? And who else do we know to have (as in the example of "Safe in Their Alabaster Chambers") so effectively advised her on the composition of poems? Certainly not Higginson. Sue was Dickinson's surrogate for survival in a world of psychic concessions. Her perceptive criticism of the "Alabaster" poem (and doubtless others), her connubial possession of Austin (the poet's closest male ally), her ability to become the *real* "belle" of Amherst – indeed, the remarkable way she had "linearized" her life – made Sue the most interesting person in Dickinson's life. Whatever the cause of the rift between them, we know (1) that it coincided with Ned's birth and (2) that it lasted with various degrees of intensity for the next fifteen to twenty years. On the surface, it may have been due to the fact that in-laws inevitably quarrel or that close neighbors finally trespass on each other's privacy. But the quarrel ran deeper than that, for Sue was no longer willing to serve as Emily's surrogate – in either the psychological or social sense. She was now asserting herself as something more than an in-law or a neighbor. No more the poet's surrogate for survival, Sue became a Dickinson in her own right – and as such the matriarch and mother that Dickinson told Higginson she never had.

The distance between the two houses on Main Street widened considerably in the 1860s. The warmth of their youthful affection, when they shared the promises of youth and adolescence, was now consigned to the "alabaster chamber" of experience. "I am not suited dear Emily with the second verse," Sue told the poet in 1861 when she was searching for a second stanza for "Safe in Their Alabaster Chambers." "You never made a peer for that verse, and I *guess* you[r] kingdom does'nt hold one." All the response the poet of Amherst could manage was the meek hope that someday she might make Sue and Austin proud of her. In the meantime she sent over a crumb for the "Ring dove" – the baby Ned, whose arrival she lamented with the sigh that a little while ago there was *"just – 'Sue.' "*

In this context we can better appreciate the poet's exclamation at the close of a decade of poetry (in the 1860s) that "To miss you, Sue, is power. The stimulus of Loss makes most Possession mean." Sue's "Riches," as she had told her earlier, "taught me – poverty! / Myself a 'Millionaire.' " What Emily Dickinson discovered and investigated in poems whose composition coincided with the war that brought the American "Renaissance" to a close was the profound loneliness of man. In the wake of so many demiurgic celebrations in Emerson and Whitman, this poet found herself adrift and awash in the grim sea of silence. Life was not ameliorative or even continuous. It was discursive – indeed, as discursive as the poetry that sought to arrest it. Life was loss, and as such it was power. The surrogates filled our landscapes of memory, but it was only inside the "haunted house" of poetry that they finally served out psychic needs:

> I could not drink it, Sue,
> Till you had tasted first –
> Though cooler than the Water – was
> The Thoughtfulness of Thirst –

All lives were peopled with substitutes, but inside the house of poetry they became true surrogates. Sue had been Emily's surrogate if never, in fact, her sincere friend. Accordingly, she sent this quatrain to Sue in 1864 as a kind of thank you note. In the variorum edition of her poems, "Sue" is replaced by "Sweet" (J. 818), for sweet indeed had been Emily's transition from person to poet. Sue had been the sweet agony that brought this most un-Whitmanesque poet to her "boil" in 1861.

As a surrogate for the promises of youth and adolescence, Sue was that chimera that dramatized the power of loss. God was an "Indian giver," and Sue had been Emily's "Indian Summer." The following poem, given this title in the 1890 edition, suggests that the chimera is merely a surrogate for another chimera: "The old – old – sophistries of June":

> These are the days when Birds come back –
> A very few – a Bird or two –
> To take a backward look.
>
> These are the days when skies resume
> The old – old sophistries of June –
> A blue and gold mistake.
>
> Oh fraud that cannot cheat the Bee –
> Almost thy plausibility
> Induces my belief.

Till ranks of seeds their witness bear –
And softly thro' the altered air
Hurries a timid leaf.

Oh Sacrament of summer days,
Oh Last Communion in the Haze –
Permit a child to join.

Thy sacred emblems to partake –
Thy consecrated bread to take
And thine immortal wine!   (J. 130)

Not even the most idealistic undergraduate reader of this poem would
agree to relive life through exactly as it had been, for he already senses
that even the "summer" of our lives was not quite what we had hoped
for. We nevertheless hold onto life's central illusion: that the future or
the object of our desire is *not* "a faded song . . . / Of wistful regret for
those who are not yet here to regret." As T. S. Eliot reminds us in "The
Dry Salvages," "time is no healer." It is not linear but circular, returning
us – often painfully – to the past that had never lived up to our expectations. Surrogates, therefore, were the essence of experience. They were
the "Sacrament of summer days" that induced yet another "child's rem-
iniscence."

Attempting to characterize Dickinson's poems in 1894, Mabel Loomis
Todd wrote, "Emily Dickinson's verses, often but a reflection of a passing mood, do not always completely represent herself – rarely, indeed,
showing the dainty humor, the frolicsome gayety, which completely
bubbled over in her daily life." There is, to be sure, a "frolicsome gayety" to be noted in J. 130. The poem conjures up that fictional day when
"Birds come back" to contemplate their future plans, to take another
look before flying south. Like our surrogates, they suggest that life is
free of necessity and innocently eternal. More frolicsome is the following
poem:

A Bird came down the Walk –
He did not know I saw –
He bit an Angleworm in halves
And ate the fellow, raw,

And then he drank a Dew
From a convenient Grass –
And then hopped sidewise to the Wall
To let a Beetle pass –

He glanced with rapid eyes
That hurried all around –
They looked like frightened Beads, I thought –
He stirred his Velvet head

Like one in danger, Cautious,
I offered him a Crumb
And he unrolled his feathers
And rowed him softer home –

Than Oars divide the Ocean,
Too silver for a seam –
Or Butterflies, off Banks of Noon
Leap, plashless as they swim.   (J. 328)

The poem gives us a rather tidy reality in which the brutality of the food chain is transformed into a kind of Disneyland scenario – life without death, crisis, or real change. If there is any suggestion of danger, it comes when the human narrator offers the bird a crumb. The truth is that nature is a nice place, a pastoral scene until man blunders on stage with the full weight of his past and future. Even the idea of an Indian summer is romantic (especially with its pejorative reference to the American Indian forgotten). Free of the human analogy with the seasons of life, Indian summer suggests with its meteorological reprieve a nature that is frolicsome rather than ferocious, a warm rather than a cold pastoral. The bird who eats an angleworm also kindly steps aside "To let a Beetle pass."

In this context Mrs. Todd's hint of a less serious or at least more lighthearted poet is understandable. But it should also be remembered that this first editor of Emily Dickinson, the mistress of her brother and "personal" acquaintance of the poet for five years, never actually saw the woman she called frolicsome and gay. As an accomplished pianist, Mabel performed for Emily on many occasions in the parlor of the Homestead, but always with her auditor listening from the adjoining room. Mabel never got that close to the poems either. With greater insight she might have realized that her characterization of Dickinson's work as "the reflection of a passing mood" completely overlooked the presence of the brooding self in every otherwise "frolicsome" scene from nature. Mabel was rather permanently infatuated – in love with the idea of being in love – and as a consequence never saw Emily as any more than the eccentric if talented sister of the man she adored. Mabel was never really part of the poet's select society, but she was the mistress of one who was. She was Austin's last surrogate, the nature that frolicked until Austin came to her. No doubt the poet a hedge away smiled a little. Mabel was at the beginning of a great career, and Emily greeted her with the following poem, sent in 1882, barely a month after Austin had declared his "Rubicon":

> A Route of Evanescence
> With a revolving Wheel –
> A resonance of Emerald –
> A Rush of Cochineal –
> And every Blossom on the Bush
> Adjusts it's tumbled Head –
> The mail from Tunis, probably
> An easy Morning's Ride –   (J. 1463)

To Mabel in love, the poem must have seemed an appropriate greeting indeed. For her life *was* love. For Austin life – or Mabel – was a concubine. She was his surrogate for the thing he had lost on the way to becoming "Squire Dickinson," the treasurer and de facto president of Amherst College. Something in him had slipped away as easily as the hummingbird, and it was time for another surrogate. In fact, it was always time for surrogates. Life was loss and gain. Surrogates were, as Emily had told Sue back in 1871,

> Indemnity for Loneliness
> That such a Bliss has been.   (J. 1179)

Displaced feelings were ultimately misplaced feelings, for our only way back to that initial bliss was through the present pageant of lovers. Life was without doubt a "Route of Evanescence."

No one realized this better than Emily Dickinson. And back in the 1860s she probably had more to say about the dilemma than anyone else in America. "Forever," she began to insist, "is composed of Nows" (J. 624). Experience, past and future, consisted of the present moment or object. This *was* the real self. Dickinson would have agreed with William James, her contemporary in the quest for a usable reality, that the difference between subject and object, mind and matter, was merely functional. Our need for surrogates proved the point, for they were our only link to what we perceived to be the true and original identity of the "mind alone." We were always trying to get back to the landscape of our lives, always trying to become one with the harmonious self in nature:

> They called me to the Window, for
> " 'Twas Sunset" – Some one said –
> I only saw a Sapphire Farm –
> And just a Single Herd –

Of Opal Cattle – feeding far
Upon so vain a Hill –
As even while I looked – dissolved –
Nor Cattle were – nor Soil –

But in their Room – a Sea – displayed –
And Ships – of such a size
As Crew of Mountains – could afford –
And Decks – to seat the skies –

This – too – the Showman rubbed away –
And when I looked again –
Nor Farm – nor Opal Herd – was there –
Nor Mediterranean –   (J. 628)

This admittedly is not one of Dickinson's "strong" poems, or even one of her particularly good ones. But like the "Master" letters, it provides a few clues to her psychic dilemma. Like Whitman's woman "aft the blinds," who longs to join the twenty-eight naturally attired male bathers, Dickinson's persona in this poem longs for the baptismal or life-giving experience. The observer is always called to the window of her room on the second story of life, but only to be displaced from the object of desire. The first look is the last look. When Dickinson's protagonist "looked again," the window failed her. Experience is fleeting, and only through the second story of art can she look again.

In 1862 Emily told Sue in a poem that even though experience (and the self) could not be fully penetrated by the observer,

At least – it solaces – to know –
That there *exists* – a *Gold* –
Altho' I prove it, just in time –
It's distance – to behold!
It's far – far – Treasure – to surmise
And estimate – the Pearl –
That slipped – my simple fingers – thro'
While yet a Girl – at School!   (J. 299)

One of her earlier biographers suggests that the poem was composed on the ninth anniversary of the death of Benjamin Franklin Newton, one of the poet's first "mentors" and certainly a surrogate for experience. Appropriately, the poem was sent to Sue, another "mentor" and surrogate. It matters little, of course, who the particular subject was – Newton or Sue. The important point is that the poem records that memorable first experience with Experience. There indeed *"exists – a Gold,"* its existence proved by its elusive nature. Dickinson's discovery nine years after Newton's death and at the height of her poetic vision was that the illusion was superior to the reality, the surrogate more real than the illusive reality it represented.

Naturally, Sue was now more important than Newton, who himself had doubtless become more important than the person he replaced, probably the poet's retiring father, who in turn had displaced her ailing mother. Sue was merely another surrogate, but the parallel role she played in Dickinson's adolescence and the timing of her departure made her the catalyst the poet required:

> Ourselves were wed one summer – dear –
> Your Vision – was in June –
> And when Your little Lifetime failed,
> I wearied – too – of mine –

The poem concludes:

> 'Tis true, Your Garden led the Bloom,
> For mine – in Frosts – was sown,
> And yet, one Summer, we were Queens –
> But You – were crowned in June –   (J. 631)

By 1862 Sue had "died" and gone to heaven next door – to a domesticity that Emily could never accept for herself. Up to that time they had been "Queens" together in the sense of having the normal expectations about life. Sue had bloomed in June when all good brides were "crowned." But Emily's adolescence, as it were, came to term in the Indian summer of her life – when the illusions were surely better than the reality. She had given a great deal of herself to Sue in the past decade, and now it all came back to her in the form of Experience. That is to say, she could in 1862 more clearly apprehend the life she was trying to authenticate in her poems – the life that was, like the hummingbird in "A Route of Evanescence," always leaving before the poem was finished. "You see I remember," she told Sue in the letter that accompanied the elegy composed on the anniversary of Newton's death. Surrogates were all we ever had; the present embodied the bodiless past. Sue had served not only as another surrogate for the past or "summer" but as *the* surrogate for the "old – old sophistries of June." With Sue's domestication and desertion, Emily was surely "afoot" with her vision.

It becomes even clearer* why the poet turned in her Indian summer to Thomas Wentworth Higginson. After Sue, Dickinson needed no more

---

*See my earlier discussion, pp. 20–3.

surrogates as literary arbiters. She would come to the world now as a poet instead of a sister or sister-in-law. She would welcome the disinterested reader who found only the "supposed person" in her poems. Higginson was the ideal reader. He would find nothing personal in the poetry because their relationship was not much more than a business agreement. "Because you have much business, beside[s] the growth of me," she told him at the outset in 1862, "you will appoint, yourself, how often I shall come – without your inconvenience. And if at any time – you regret you received me, or I prove a different fabric to that you supposed – you must banish me." We can hardly imagine the poet treating Sue so distantly, but Emily was Higginson's "scholar," not his "lover." She really had nothing to lose with him and everything to gain.

With this letter to Higginson, Emily Dickinson removed herself "as the Representative of [her] Verse." And it is significant that she did so at the close of a two-year period in which she wrote the best poetry of her life. She was ready to make Austin and Sue "proud" of her – but as a "public" poet and not as a private person or "lover." She would not publish, of course, but she would expose enough of her work to become *known* as a poet. She would establish an identity outside of the family, so to speak – outside of the marriage of Austin and Sue. This she accomplished through Higginson, for though he was no outspoken champion of Dickinson's, he was bewildered enough to speak of her work to others, including that most public of poets, Helen Hunt Jackson.

Dickinson launched her secret career wisely, and before long had Jackson and others begging to publish her work. A clue to her strategy is found in the poems she included in her business-like letter to Higginson. By and large they were pieces that evoked her detachment from the brooding and bruised self that Sue had known. That is to say, they removed that self from the nature or experience they described. "He defeated – dying," for example, in "Success Is Counted Sweetest" (J. 67) is reduced to the "supposed person." We are so far removed from the field of battle in the poem as to suggest that failure (and the grave) is intended for somebody else. Another enclosed in the letter was "Some Keep the Sabbath Going to Church" (J. 324). Here as in "These Are the Days When Birds Come Back" the human concern over the past and future is muted by songs of innocence. The problem of a religious vocation, once an overwhelming dilemma for Dickinson, is relegated to the simplicity of non-human nature:

> With a Bobolink for a Chorister –
> And an Orchard, for a Dome

The narrator may be whistling in the dark but nevertheless whistling. He keeps the Sabbath with himself, even though a little fearful of where that course of action is taking him:

So instead of getting to Heaven, at last –
I'm going, all along.

In neither poem does Dickinson allow the narrator to take the scene into the silence that characterizes her poems of personal crisis, such as "The Soul Selects Her Own Society" (J. 303) and "My Life Had Stood – a Loaded Gun" (J. 754).

The same can be said for "Your Riches – Taught Me – Poverty" (J. 299) and "Of Tribulation – These Are They" (J. 325), also sent to Higginson. Both appear to offer domestic security. They cheer up the pilgrim on the way home to the self, a self that is *called back* from the brink of annihilation:

> But we – stood – whispering in the House –
> And all we said – was
>   SAVED!   (J. 325)

Parts of J. 299, it has been noted, echo the sentimentality found in Longfellow's *Kavanagh* (1849). We know, of course, that the poem was sent to Sue, and in this regard it was intended as a personal statement. But even here it was sent after the special relationship between the poet and Sue had ruptured in 1862; hence, its sentiments were as sentimental as those of *Kavanagh* and the work of such female writers who labored under the tutelage of Higginson. Just as public is the sentiment in J. 325, where " 'Surrender' – is a sort unknown" and " 'Defeat', an Outgrown Anguish." This was palaver for public consumption: Victory is supposedly found in the Christian version of defeat. William Dean Howells would warm to the same idea in *The Rise of Silas Lapham* (1885). No doubt Higginson read the poems as yet another version of terror with a happy ending, victory of the human spirit over the human condition.

Dickinson was playing the literary market with Higginson. That August she sent him two poems that not only appealed to the conventional critic's need for order in a chaotic world but even had a recognizable story line. With "I Cannot Dance upon My Toes" (J. 326) and "Before I Got My Eye Put Out" (J. 327), she expressed the hope that they were "more orderly" than the ones previously sent. She added that she had never had a "Monarch" in her life and "cannot rule myself." Both poems can be read as statements of spiritual victory over mortal circumstances: that one can *order* himself in the face of adversity. Dickinson knew, of course, what Faulkner taught us in this century: that art is the product of "the human heart in conflict with itself." She hinted as much in her ploy to Higginson, almost as if to apologize if he should discern the real subject of the poems. "When I try to organize," she told him, "my little Force explodes – and leaves me bare and charred." In one sense, a recent feminist argument is correct in observing that Dickinson's persona is that naughty little girl who refuses to grow up and follow the Sues of the world next door. She would remain in her room on the second story, all the while insisting on her vision of the human condition. As she confessed in her third "Master" letter, written that year and very likely addressed to exponents of conventional wisdom such as Higginson, "Daisy knows all that – but she must go unpardoned."

In "I Cannot Dance upon My Toes," the protagonist reveals an extended knowledge of an art she cannot perform – ballet. Could she dance, she would perform "In Pirouette to blanch a Troupe – / Or lay a Prima, mad." Her special vocabulary belies her statement that she lacks "Ballet knowledge." In fact, she knows the art so well that her pirouette would astonish as much as the "revolving Wheel" of the hummingbird. The poem observes the paradox of experience – the gap between knowing and doing *anything*. She "cannot dance upon [her] Toes" the way she can in her mind, where surrogates for actual experience perform the impossible. This poem, as with many of her others, expresses the anxiety of knowing. "Nor any know I know the Art / I mention – easy – Here," she concludes in the final stanza. In other words, she knows the "Art" so well precisely because she cannot perform it. Like the dying person in "Success Is Counted Sweetest," the "distant strains of triumph" are agonizingly clear. Life's mandatory distance from the prize is itself the very quality of life, for the nature of experience is finally a knowledge of absence. As with the landscape in J. 328, once we attempt to "stage" our dreams or enter the scene we envision, it disappears like the "troupe" blanched out of existence by the vicarious ballerina's pirouette.

It has been observed in Chapter 1 that "Before I Got My Eye Put Out" marks the point in Dickinson's career when she stopped looking for life and started listening to it. That was all the serious student of experience could ever do: "Guess – with just my soul / Upon the Window pane." Once again the protagonist is brought to the window – in order to hear now but not see the bathers whose number in Whitman's poem denotes the cycle of experience. Just as the ballerina cannot dance, the narrator of J. 327 cannot see what she knows exists just below her window. Both poems (J. 326 and 327) underscore the paradoxical nature of knowledge, for the window in this one – like the stage in the other – can accommodate only the disembodied self. The body that Whitman would have soused with the "spray" of the twenty-eight bathers is left at the windowsill, for the house of nature in Dickinson's ontology has no doors – only windows.

Windows abound in Dickinson's poetry, but the most arresting use of them occurs in "I Heard a Fly Buzz – When I Died" (J. 465). It may be a measure of the psychological inadequacy of our society a hundred years hence that air conditioning has led to the disappearance of windows in public buildings. That is to say, our windowless existence mocks the notion that human nature is somehow liberated through technology. We are as locked away in the house of nature as were our antecedents in the nineteenth century – perhaps more so because our "interior" windows literally fail with a power shortage. We can instantly become the victims of our own invention. This dilemma may give us a special insight into Dickinson's poem about the *housefly*. In her own screenless day the window let in more than just the light:

> There interposed a Fly –
> With Blue – uncertain stumbling Buzz –
> Between the light – and me –
> And then the Windows failed – and then
> I could not see to see –

The fly is the last thing the dying person *sees*. It is not that it literally blocks out the light and brings on darkness; rather, darkness is the result of the windowless condition that accompanies death – indeed, *is* death. Life is a house with windows that allow us a view of the human condition. When those windows fail, we die or at best become isolated within our own fantasies about the progress of the human race. We are guided by *tech*nology and not knowledge. This poem, like the one about the ballerina, is about the high cost of knowledge. As Dickinson wrote elsewhere, it is knowing that life is not what we thought it was:

> I cannot live with You –
> It would be Life –
> And Life is over there –
> Behind the Shelf   (J. 640)

Of course, "I Heard a Fly Buzz" is about literal death as well, but that is not its most important theme. In fact, many of Dickinson's poems about death have been analyzed too literally. For Dickinson, death is always a metaphor for experience, because life is always measured by its loss. Our windows are always in danger of failing, and this is what brings us most closely in touch with ourselves. When we are benumbed by the technology of a windowless existence, we are shut off from ourselves and the life that really matters. We are left at the mercy of the common housefly that invades even air-conditioned spaces and whose importance and certainly capacity to irritate are utterly minimized in the nature outside the windows of ourselves.

"The eye is the first circle," Emerson wrote; "the horizon which it forms is the second; and throughout nature this primary figure is repeated without end." He calls the eye in "Circles" the "highest emblem in the cipher of the world." Dickinson, who doubtless read the essay, would have agreed, but she would have also protested that it was the window to a world that we could not possess. Every time she began to follow that cipher up Emerson's stairway of surprise, she heard a fly buzz. The eye was the first circle and the last circle. It was what we used to call the "picture" window. It provided a view and nothing more, but without it life was a windowless existence. In this sense, critics such as Anderson are correct to observe that the poem is about the anticlimactic nature of death. Instead of witnessing "the King . . . in the Room," the protagonist hears (and *sees* for the last time) the "uncertain stumbling Buzz" of a bluebottle. Death, like life, never quite lives up to its billing.

Life consisted of impossible situations made nearly possible by surrogates. "Remoteness is the founder of sweetness," Emily told her Norcross cousins in 1873. "Could we see all we hope, or hear the whole we fear told tranquil, like another tale, there would be madness near. Each of us gives or takes heaven in corporeal persons, for each of us has the skill of life." Life's skill lay in never venturing beyond the window in pursuit of fulfillment but remaining back with its surrogates:

> One need not be a Chamber – to be Haunted –
> One need not be a House –
> The Brain has Corridors – surpassing
> Material Place –
>
> Far safer, of a Midnight Meeting
> External Ghost
> Than it's interior Confronting –
> That Cooler Host.
>
> Far safer, through an Abbey gallop,
> The Stone a'chase –
> Than Unarmed, one's a'self encounter –
> In lonesome Place –
>
> Ourself behind ourself, concealed –
> Should startle most –
> Assassin hid in our Apartment
> Be Horror's least.
>
> The Body – borrows a Revolver –
> He bolts the Door –
> O'erlooking a superior spectre –
> Or More –   (J. 670)

One was always seeking a coda to the song of himself. The object of this final lovesong was not to be found, however, in the haunted house of another (lover) but within the self that was haunted with the surrogates of a lover that could never be. Each surrogate showed us "Ourself behind ourself, concealed." The search for that lover always led to the startling discovery of ourselves.

When her nephew died in 1883, Emily Dickinson imagined a child anxiously waiting to go outside: " 'Open the Door, open the Door, they are waiting for me,' was Gilbert's sweet command in delirium. *Who* were waiting for him, all we possess we would give to know." All we ever knew, she knew by then and long before, was that life was bounded by love and death and peopled with surrogates. Gilbert ran out of the house and into "the little Grave at his Grandparents' feet." Life was love and death: death of a love and love of the dead in the image of its surrogate. Dickinson might have said with Whitman, "As to you Life I reckon you are the leavings of many deaths." But this was the only life that mattered – that consisting of surrogates for what we once were and wanted to become again. With each of these lovers we strove ever and anon to discover the "wing'd purposes" of ourselves:

> Cocoon above! Cocoon below!
> Stealthy Cocoon, why hide you so
> What all the world suspect?
> An hour, and gay on every tree
> Your secret, perched in extasy
> Defies imprisonment!
>
> An hour in Chrysalis to pass,
> Then gay above receding grass
> A Butterfly to go!
> A moment to interrogate,
> Then wiser than a "Surrogate,"
> The Universe to know!   (J. 129)

Much was promised, but all that was ever revealed – the poet perhaps knew at the death of young Gilbert – was the father of Father Emerson and Emily.

Chapter 5

IN MEDIAS RES

Of all the unwritten scenes in American literature, surely the greatest is that in which Hester Prynne tells Arthur Dimmesdale that she is pregnant with his child. For in *The Scarlet Letter,* whose overriding theme is the power of guilt, the reader is plunged into the middle of a drama that begins with an illicit act of sexual intercourse. Indeed, the act is so illicit for the circumstances that we can hardly imagine Hester and Arthur actually *doing it.* The tale begins *in medias res* – that is, with Hester's "open ignominy." We encounter Hawthorne's Adam and Eve after they have heard the Voice in the Garden and have realized their nakedness. Although Dimmesdale manages to remain in hiding, the judgment or "penance" has already been rendered. The Rev. Wilson addresses "to the multitude a discourse on sin, in all its branches, but with continual reference to the ignominious letter." It is the letter "A," of course, but it stands for "Adam" as well as for "adultery."

The scene begins Dimmesdale as well as the novel *in medias res,* for Hawthorne's character is really born, as we all are, in the illicit act of life itself – or "sin, in all its branches." In this "second story" to Hawthorne's masterpiece, we would have Dimmesdale's true shock of recognition, his sense of shame and fear upon learning of Hester's condition. What would ensue, as it ensues with the facts of the human condition, is the guilt over having lived that moment of ecstasy and the fear of its consequences. One is tempted here (in a book about Dickinson instead of Hawthorne) to conjure up J. 125, where we are told that "For each extatic instant / We must an anguish pay." But the poem has a lugubrious ring in this context, for that abiding sense of guilt is somehow missing. In the poem it is as if we had *earned* the ecstasies with our anguishes, had paid dearly for them many times over:

> For each beloved hour
> Sharp pittances of years –

> Bitter contested farthings –
> And Coffers heaped with Tears!

Dickinson in this instance is playing Emerson's game of compensation. This is the relatively early Dickinson, the twenty-nine-year-old poet who might resemble the twenty-eight-year-old Edna Pontillier as she ponders Emerson in *The Awakening*. Both have yet to awake to the life of surrogates and illusions. Another "second story" in American literature, of course, would be Edna's sense of guilt after sleeping with Arobin. But the fact that guilt is altogether missing from Chopin's novel is probably what keeps it from being rightfully proclaimed a masterpiece. Edna has been wronged as Melville thought he had been – and so feels "spotless as a lamb" with regard to her actions.

The protagonist in the poems of Emily Dickinson, however, is far more complicated. Like Hawthorne's Adam *out* of the Garden, the "supposed person" is both wronged and not wronged enough for living. With Dimmesdale, he would say, "Of penance I have had enough! Of penitence there has been none!" This is because our sense of life, our psychic pain, begins *in medias res*. As the older Amherst poet wrote:

> Pain – has an Element of Blank –
> It cannot recollect
> When it begun – or if there were
> A time when it was not –

The misuse of the pluperfect in the third line reinforces the sense of life's beginning *in medias res,* or after the Fall. Before we did not know we *were* naked. Rather than follow Edna into the sea of despair or Dimmesdale upon the moonlit scaffold, Dickinson grew up to confront the guilt that follows – indeed stalks as the *duenna* counting her beads does Chopin's two lovers on the beach – every moment of ecstasy:

> It has no Future – but itself –
> It's Infinite contain
> It's Past – enlightened to perceive
> New Periods – of Pain.   (J. 650)

Life is like illicit love – the "Wild Nights" of our days. Its true sense is adulterous, for it is what should never be. "I cannot live with You," we will recall the poet's saying in J. 640

> It would be Life –
> And Life is over there –
> Behind the Shelf.

Life is as illogical as the phrase "Behind the Shelf." Yet its illusive quality is what makes it both attractive and repulsive. For Life is, as the more mature Dickinson discovered, somehow exactly what we do not want. As a consequence, Dickinson's concept of life is exactly the opposite of Emerson's theory of compensation. The notion of balance animates both theories, but Dickinson's emphasis is upon the loss rather than the gain in nature. In other words, the bad not only offsets the good but also makes possible our sense of ratio. One could not return to the Garden because it was still the "Cold Pastoral" of loss and gain. The poet tells her lover that she could never live with him:

> Nor could I rise – with You –
> Because Your Face
> Would put out Jesus' –
> That New Grace

"That New Grace" was the disembodied lover who never took us beyond the point of desire. Like the lovers in Keats's "Ode," we all expected what we could never have. We wanted the New Eden, but it was quite impossible to leave behind the Old World of the finite self:

> Me from Myself – to banish –
> Had I Art –
> Invincible my Fortress
> Unto All Heart –
>
> But since Myself – assault Me –
> How have I peace
> Except by subjugating
> Consciousness?
>
> And since We're mutual Monarch
> How this be
> Except by Abdication –
> Me – of Me?   (J. 642)

It was the assault of the quotidian self that kept her from those sublime moments of Emersonian confidence. Dickinson kept falling into the consciousness of her own nakedness. She kept falling into the middle of her life – *in medias res*. Like Hawthorne's dilemma with Dimmesdale, it was the only half she knew. The other half, the self that like Dimmesdale had dwelled in the Eden of experience (and the one that Emerson would have us return to), was simply unutterable. One could not even begin to know that happier self – what Keats called the "more happy, happy love!" – "Except by Abdication."

In other words, there was no "Second Coming" of the self. It is little wonder then that the young poet-to-be could not follow her classmates in accepting Christ as her "lover." She could not because "It would be Life" (J. 640), and life was irrevocably linked with death. Her lover would not have been God – but the son of God, the one who had to die in order to live in the lives of all those Amherst Christians who believed in a domestic heaven. "Come slowly – Eden!" (J. 211) the poet warns, for the Wall of Flames, she knew, was a wall of guilt. No pagan to its density could ever break through. And yet no one could touch the initial self without getting his fingers burned from possession.

Only solitude of the first order could have produced this version and vision of the self. Dickinson's was the result of no pilgrimage from society *to* solitude. No child ever "went forth" in her pageant of lovers. It was from beginning to end the solitary self *in medias res*. Her vision is almost Poesque in its *doppelganger* drama. She awakes in the middle of the night in the gothic mansion of the self – already formed and destined to roam its haunted corridors. "Each life," Dickinson tells us in J. 680, "Converges to some Centre – / Expressed or still." It is the center that is everywhere and nowhere:

> Embodied scarcely to itself – it may be –
> Too fair
> For Credibility's presumption
> To mar –

The credible presumption is the fiction that life has a beginning, middle, and end – when in truth it has only a middle. It is a moving center and a moving target that leaves us always with Dickinson's famous "Loaded Gun." We are always at the center and never, in the sense of wanting to get back to where Hawthorne could not begin with Dimmesdale. Life as we perceive it always began with a clear sense of nakedness. It was finally somehow illicit, as if we were God's bye-blow – and the guilt derived from that beginning was the driving force in our lives. It pitted the self against the self, or as Dickinson puts it:

> The Soul unto itself
> Is an imperial friend –
> Or the most agonizing Spy –
> An Enemy – could send   (J. 683)

She goes on to say in the poem that it is "Secure against it's own," but also admits that it is "Sovereign – of itself." The phrases recall Plato's consideration of "the master of oneself" dilemma in *The Republic*. He calls it an absurd phrase: "For if you're master *of* yourself you're presumably also subject *to* yourself, and so *both* master *and* subject. For there is only one person in question throughout." His solution is to balance all those conflicting impulses or selves, but any student of Plato knows it is a system of equality in which the so-called rational parts are "more equal" than the irrational ones. Such a utopia of the mind would have been too Emersonian for Dickinson, whose days were punctuated with too many wild nights. Like Whitman's utopia of the self that allows for the passions instead of suppressing them, Dickinson's "second story" allowed for an equality of the self that always verged upon anarchy. She found herself ever and anon in the middle of the conflict – having never known peace and never expecting it. Her business, as she told Higginson, was indeed "Circumference," but it was a circumference that zeroed in on that ever-moving center of her life.

In "The First Day That I Was a Life" (J. 902), Dickinson notes in her posthumous voice that both the first and last days were still. And even though the first was "full" and the last "empty," she cannot decide which day she prefers:

> "Which choose I"?
> That – I cannot say –
> "Which choose They"?
> Question Memory!

Memory, in fact, *is* circumference, for it projects the past upon the future and so frames the life. It is the eye of the present which draws the beginning and the end into the middle. And just as we find ourselves *in medias res,* so the poets find and leave the world that way:

> The Poets light but Lamps –
> Themselves – go out –
> The Wicks they stimulate –
> If vital Light
>
> Inhere as do the Suns –
> Each Age a Lens
> Disseminating their
> Circumference –   (J. 883)

By the time we come to appreciate the "vital Light," the poet has departed and left us to encounter him *in medias res.* His art awakes us to something in our primordial experience. Ultimately, we discover in the poet's work what we discover about lives: that they began, as it were, without us. As Whitman wrote in the song of *him*self:

> Before I was born out of my mother generations guided me,
> My embryo has never been torpid, nothing could overlay it.

Whitman knew what Dickinson knew (and may have learned from Whitman): that we sleep through "the lethargic mist" to awaken in the center of our lives. "All forces," Whitman writes, "have been steadily employ'd to complete and delight me / Now on this spot I stand with my robust soul." Dickinson herself proclaims:

> Before Myself was born
> 'Twas settled, so they say,
> A Territory for the Ghosts –
> And Squirrels, formerly.

The lines are taken from J. 892, a poem that reminds us of Frost's "Stopping by Woods on a Snowy Evening," at least in its opening lines:

> Who occupies this House?
> A Stranger I must judge
> Since No one knows his Circumstance –
> 'Tis well the name and age
>
> Are writ upon the Door
> Or I should fear to pause
> Where not so much as Honest Dog
> Approach encourages.

The poet encounters the house of the self in a ghost town but one that is eventually resettled:

> And from a Settlement
> A Capitol has grown
> Distinguished for the gravity
> Of every Citizen.

The speaker awakes to the society of the self, and yet it is haunted by that one house whose owner – like the owner of Frost's snow-filled wood – also owns him, or his past, for all that can really be known is the present:

> The Owner of this House
> A Stranger He must be –
> Eternity's Acquaintances
> Are mostly so – to me.

We might return to Dimmesdale's dilemma to inquire into the identity of Dickinson's "Owner," for Dimmesdale's dilemma was also Dickinson's. That is to say, they both discover in their search for the past the serpent in the Garden. It was, of course, the "narrow Fellow in the Grass" who tempted Dimmesdale as well as Dickinson, tempted him to reclaim his origins in the Garden. Both awake, however, to find Eden a ghost town. In *The Scarlet Letter* Arthur Dimmesdale never gets any closer to

Hester Prynne than Adam got to Eve in the Book of Genesis. In both cases, they *awake* to their guilt and their nakedness before God. It was always life *in medias res*. It left the fictional Dimmesdale flaccid and the real Dickinson fecund but lost in "a curious Town" in which "Some Houses [were] very old" and "Some – newly raised this Afternoon" (J. 892). Life, as she taught us, is an Eden of plausibility without possibility. In order to create – to return to the Garden and its owner – we return not only to God (in the sense of being "creators") but to the guilt that informs all existence, to the Original Sin of the self. In Dickinson's words, we cannot enter the garden of our existence or go beyond the point of desire without encountering the serpent Guilt – "the narrow Fellow in the Grass":

> You may have met Him – did you not
> His notice sudden is –
>
> The Grass divides as with a Comb –
> A spotted shaft is seen –
> And then it closes at your feet
> And opens further on –

According to the Genesis myth, "the serpent was more subtil than any beast of the field which the Lord God had made." From all of "Nature's People" the poet felt "a transport / Of Cordiality –"

> But never met this Fellow
> Attended, or alone
> Without a tighter breathing
> And Zero at the Bone –   (J. 986)

It was the one beast of the jungle that could not be soothed by the artist's lyre.

Like Dimmesdale in the Dark Wood, the poet was always doing sufficient penance but never enough penitence for the Original Sin of the self. This was the fable Dickinson told over and over in her poems: that man kept waking up in the New World of himself as "a Boy and Barefoot." Life was like "a Whip lash / Unbraiding in the Sun" – come and gone in a flash, "wrinkled, and was gone." It is difficult to understand how the editors of her day could have dubbed the poem "The Snake" instead of "The Serpent," at least. Shorn of its biblical illusions, the poem supposes no *person* at all; it becomes simply another "Nature" poem, catalogued that way in the 1891 edition. Rightly read, it reduces our vision of the Garden of Eden to "a Boggy Acre." This was Dickinson's circumference and her business – to follow life back to that "Zero at the

Bone," to center upon the fact and consequence of existence. Man was alienated from the Eden of himself, lost in the New World of the self. Like Dimmesdale in the Dark Wood with his Hester, he always hoped to return to the bliss of the initial self – indeed, to escape there. But as Hawthorne knew, he could never get past the serpent, or his guilt over having lived. Later, American writers with utopian tendencies such as Hamlin Garland might allow us our return "up the coule," but there was no homecoming for Hawthorne's supposed minister or Dickinson's "supposed person." Like Emerson's Central Man after the Fall, he found himself at the center of nowhere.

In Chapter 3 we observed that the narrator of "My Life Had Stood – a Loaded Gun" (J. 754) is an inanimate object. As such it suggests the disembodied voice of the poem itself, which remains loaded but inanimate until we start reading – or shooting. Until we exercise "the power to kill," the poem cannot give us "the power to die." That is to say, to read is to write a part of ourselves into the oblivion of eternity – out of the particular and into the general life that respects nothing "corporeal." With great poetry we come to life, to the consciousness of our frailty as "corporeal friend[s]." That life began when man was cast out of the Garden, and he has been *dying* to return ever since. God created us by killing off our bliss, by clearing away "the lethargic mist." Now "We roam in Sovreign Woods," lured there by the Voice in the Garden that comes to us as a mere echo of our own voice:

> And every time I speak for Him –
> The Mountains straight reply –

The voice of God is our own voice because, as Dickinson suggests, God speaks through us, not to us. No wonder her poems go off into the silence: because that is where God is, both east of Eden and west of Eden – indeed, at all points on the circumference of our center.

If her business was circumference, as Dickinson told Higginson, it was also necessarily the center or middle of things. In other words, one was a dilation of the other. God was an expansion of the self, an inflation of the I or ego to its bursting point – or back to the Fall of Man. We were God once and wanted to be again, but instead we were always finding ourselves in the Dark Wood with Hester, telling her of our guilt. We were Dante without our Virgil. We could not *begin* to find our way back to the Garden, much less penetrate its Wall of Flames. Touched by God in the sense that language is freedom from the material world of necessity, we were nevertheless always being cast – or kept – out of the Garden. Or as Dickinson writes of her "supposed person":

> To this World she returned.
> But with a tinge of that –
> A Compound manner,
> As a Sod
> Espoused a Violet,
> That chiefer to the Skies
> Than to Himself, allied,
> Dwelt hesitating, half of Dust,
> And half a Day, the Bride.   (J. 830)

According to Thomas H. Johnson, this poem was sent to a friend of the poet who was seriously wounded by a pistol shot intended for her maid. The friend almost died but ultimately recovered. No doubt Dickinson saw the incident as a measure of life itself: We were always being shot by the loaded gun of our desire for Eden – wounded grievously and dying a little, but ultimately recovering.

This was Dickinson's dialectic: half a day the bride and half a day in dust:

> Heavenly Hurt, it gives us –
> We can find no scar,
> But internal difference,
> Where the Meanings, are – ·   (J. 258)

Our "imperial affliction," she knew, was that "certain Slant of light" that shone down upon us from the Eden of our existence. It is probably no coincidence that the symbol of Hester's offense is also the first letter of the alphabet. The scarlet letter is the *sign* for the beginning that Hawthorne could not write about in his novel. Dickinson, too, starts in the middle when she talks about her life as *having stood*. The "Meanings" were in the middle of a life whose first and last days, she suggests, were the same. The first is "full" and the last "empty" – the fully loaded and unloaded gun. The first is inanimate and the last is inanimate. Only the middle lives, in response to the guilt emanating from the beginning and the punishment expected at the end. In other words, we feel guilty about living and fearful about dying. As Dickinson rightly asks, who could ever really choose? Between guilt and fear stood the life, pulled into the center to be recollected:

> The first Day that I was a Life
> I recollect it – How still –
> The last Day that I was a Life
> I recollect it – as well –   (J. 902)

Life was a "recollection" of the crime and the punishment, the beginning and the end. Caught in the middle or center, life was indeed involved in the business of "Circumference."

A poem that sums up man's sense of guilt without agonizing over it is one written in the 1880s:

> Of God we ask one favor,
> That we may be forgiven –
> For what, he is presumed to know –
> The Crime, from us, is hidden –
> Immured the whole of Life
> Within a magic Prison
> We reprimand the Happiness
> That too competes with Heaven   (J. 1601)

The final two lines remind us of the jealous God described in J. 1719 who

> . . . cannot bear to see
> That we had rather not with Him
> But with each other play.

The word "play" is used in more than fifty of Dickinson's poems. "We play at Paste"; "She died at play"; "Let's play those – never come!" It is synonymous with "release" – from the life of crime and punishment. Like Shakespeare's characters in such festive comedies as *A Midsummer Night's Dream* or *As You Like It,* the Dickinsonian protagonists go for a romp in the forest. They dwell not only in the Dark Wood of Dimmesdale but also in the enchanted forest of Oberon and Titania. Their "Crime" is that they find God – or at least His demands upon them – a little boring at times and thus escape into the adolescence that is present in every stage of life. Not long after Dickinson began writing poetry, she told her brother Austin, "I wish we were children now. I wish we were *always* children, how to grow up I dont know."

Adam and Eve played in the Garden and were condemned to "reprimand the Happiness / That too competes with Heaven." In another poem written about the same time, she asks: "Is Heaven an Exchequer? / They speak of what we owe" (J. 1270). We would like to think of this poet reading *The Adventures of Huckleberry Finn* (as we would like to think of her reading *Leaves of Grass*) and silently applauding the child who was good when he was bad, the child who in spite of his upbringing is not a party to "that negotiation." In other words, life was a system of emotional exchanges, transactions that were best suggested by economic exchanges. Nigger Jim, for example, receives forty dollars for being Tom's "prisoner." And that sum replaces the same amount offered by the slave catchers who in turn were attempting to assuage their sense of guilt by paying for it.

In Dickinson's world, "Heaven" is indeed an exchequer that levies a high tariff on our emotional baggage. It requires

> The slow exchange of Hope
> For something passiver – Content   (J. 652)

It was finally too expensive to get everything through the customhouse. Hope of relief was excess baggage. What got through was not Hawthorne's – or Melville's – "NO! in thunder" but Dickinson's "content" with the human condition. That is, dying and going to heaven (or back to the prelapsarian self) consisted of living with the paradoxes of the human dilemma. The pilgrim was finally content to make those emotional exchanges – to do penance for penitence.

Dickinson's pilgrim or protagonist is always having to come back from the "Midsummer – in the Mind" (J. 646) to do penance for released time. After a lifetime of such returns, of course, even "A Prison," as she tells us in J. 652, "gets to be a friend":

> We come to look with gratitude
> For the appointed Beam
> It deal us – stated as our food –
> And hungered for – the same –
>
> We learn to know the Planks –
> That answer to Our feet –
> So miserable a sound – at first –
> Nor even now – so sweet –
>
> As plashing in the Pools –
> When Memory was a Boy –
> But a Demurer Circuit
> A Geometric Joy –

He always found himself back in prison, not at all sure of what his crime had been. All he knew finally was what Jack Henry Abbott knew after almost twenty years of adult life in prison – that the existence had transformed his needs "into creatures that stalk you with reflections of every flaw in your personal existence." Abbott's case, as unique in its literary outcome as it is unfortunate in its personal consequence, is perhaps a useful gloss to Dickinson's poem and *her* version of "prison life." If the facts are stated correctly in the excerpted letters to Norman Mailer, Abbott was imprisoned initially for the hapless crime of being an abandoned child who was unable to adapt himself to foster homes and subsequently "murdered himself" into a life sentence in prison. For Dickinson "prison life" began in the same soporific fashion – "When Memory was a Boy." Life began with personal needs that had to be institutionalized as flaws in the character of the self. They were evidence of the Original and Unreasonable Sin – that initial act in the unconscious that landed us repeatedly in life's quandary and its quagmire.

The crime was personal and not "collective." Only the punishment was collective in the sense that we were deprived of our individual romp in the Garden and sentenced to the institution. We could exist only in the general, never again in the particular (which in prison is merely solitary confinement). The particular now was nothing more than Whitman's "huge first Nothing." "I know I was even there," he insists. Dickinson would agree but also protest with the question, "Are you – Nobody – too?" (J. 288). We can almost imagine such a dialogue between America's two greatest poets, the one insisting on the beauty of the particular life and the other on the truth of the general:

> And so, as Kinsmen, met a Night –
> We talked between the Rooms –
> Until the Moss had reached our lips –
> And covered up – our names –   (J. 449)

Life was a "magic Prison" that had been once a prism for that "certain Slant of light."

That light reached us now through a wintry haze – in the middle of our lives, on "Winter Afternoons." And

> When it comes, the Landscape listens –
> Shadows – hold their breath –
> When it goes, 'tis like the Distance
> On the look of Death –

Those long New England winters had their impact on Emily Dickinson. "What care the Dead for Winter?" she asked in another poem (J. 592). Winter was in the middle with the living. The dead could "Themselves as easy freeze – / June Noon – as January Night." The living huddled by the fire and speculated. They thought about "Those fair – fictitious People" who had been "plucked away / From our familiar Lifetime" (J. 499). Lost in the middle, they wondered hopefully about the end, wondered if it might be like the beginning, which they could not quite remember.

In fact, it all seemed fictitious, beautiful but as frozen over as a New England winter. Everything fair was fictitious. We lived in memory of the beginning that was in fact a "huge first Nothing" – in fact a fiction. As far as we *really* knew, everything but the middle was a fiction. The past as well as the future was a manifestation and a projection of the present. When we thought about the dead in our past, we then wondered about our own death in the future:

> Those Boys and Girls, in Canvas –
> Who stay upon the Wall
> In Everlasting Keepsake –
> Can Anybody tell?
>
> We trust – in places perfecter –
> Inheriting Delight
> Beyond our faint Conjecture –
> Our dizzy Estimate –
>
> Remembering ourselves, we trust –
> Yet Blesseder – than We –
> Through Knowing – where We only hope –
> Receiving – where we – pray –

Ironically, our concept of the future or life after death could not negate the present self that conventional religion considers inferior to the "soul." All we had in such a future was what we had on the wall of the past: icons of our own surrogated selves.

To put the matter another way, we had faith in "Those fair – fictitious" faces on the wall. They served, or our faith in them served, as

> . . . the Pierless Bridge
> Supporting what We see
> Unto the Scene that We do not –
> Too slender for the eye
>
> It bears the Soul as bold
> As it were rocked in Steel
> With Arms of Steel at either side –
> It joins – behind the Vail
>
> To what, could We presume
> The Bridge would cease to be
> To Our far, vascillating Feet
> A first Nescessity.   (J. 915)

In the variorum edition the editor dutifully refrains from correcting the spelling of "necessity." In the manuscript of the poem the word is definitely "nescessity." It may have been purposeful on Dickinson's part, as an attempt to conflate "necessity" and "nescience," for the absence of knowledge makes faith our necessity. It is a "pierless" and "peerless" bridge back to the visible nowhere of our existence, a bridge supported only by the ego. John Roebling had already constructed the first modern suspension bridge over the Ohio River in Wheeling, West Virginia, back in 1846. At the time Dickinson was only sixteen, but she would live to see Roebling's son complete the Brooklyn Bridge in 1883. In the 1850s Whitman was crossing over to Byzantium in a ferry. Ten years later but long before Roebling as well as Hart Crane, Dickinson was attempting to span the same distance. She was reaching "behind the Vail" with the same egotistic spirit in which Whitman perceived the function of poetry in his 1855 Preface. Finally, of course, the distance back to the self – in either the past or future, which were in fact the same – was too great, and the pilgrimage was indeed a *suspended* journey.

The bridge metaphor suggests that existence is never more than half over – that we always find ourselves "Suspended in the Noon" of our lives (J. 517). We never get beyond the middle "To what, could We presume / The Bridge would cease to be." Our cosmic nescience makes the bridge both a necessity and an impossibility. Yet sailing toward Byzantium was always preferable to getting there. Better "an aged man . . . a tattered coat upon a stick" than a work of art producing art instead of life. The middle or midworld was always best. Dickinson is, as remarked earlier, Emerson's Whitman of "Wisdom." The poet of experience is grimly accommodating. More than a hundred years later, we see her clearly in the middle of our literature – between Emerson and Pound, between the ideal and the actual. Lewis Heyde has recently observed in a most clever analogy that Emerson preferred the symbol or idea, whereas Whitman "cashed in" his symbol for the body or thing it represented. Emerson kept his psychic assets liquid, whereas Whitman spent his money on things. Whitman "broke the new wood" and so is rightly placed on the side of the imagists, but Dickinson neither saved nor spent her money. She remained instead the psychic pauper, the one who only *supposed* an existence outside of the present. Always in the middle between the word and the act, she stands as well at the center of our literature.

Dimmesdale, too, exists only between the word and the act. It is the mind that never quite gets back to the matter. Suspended somewhere between head and heart, he is a stranger even to his own offspring. As Dimmesdale's "future," Pearl is indeed won (and to be won) at "a great price." The amount is finally too high for Dimmesdale, as it was for Dickinson. Her sense of future was also strangely alien, for like Dimmesdale's it was the child of the past that could not be reconstructed in the present. All that really could be recovered was the guilt. This is where we first meet Dimmesdale in *The Scarlet Letter,* and it is where we first and always encounter Emily Dickinson in her poetry. In this context we

can better appreciate the message in "The Soul Selects Her Own Society" (J. 303). The poem is unique for its pattern of regression. That is,
we have in the first stanza the "supposed person" in the present selecting
her own society. In the second we have the "supposed person" in the
past, in this case Queen Elizabeth rejecting all suitors ("Unmoved –
she notes the Chariots – pausing"). In the third and final stanza the "supposed person" is reduced to an oyster, rejecting from the ocean floor all
but one grain of sand, which the bivalve will siphon in and transform
into a pearl:*

> I've known her – from an ample nation –
> Choose One –
> Then – close the Valves of her attention –
> Like Stone –

Life was indeed a pearl at a great price.

Like the barren Elizabeth, she could finally select only herself in the
present. The movement in the poem from mind ("Soul") through person (Elizabeth) to matter (the oyster) illustrates Dickinson's response to
the human condition. With neither the Emersonian ideal nor the Whitmanesque sensation as a possibility, she could only follow her symbol
back to the seclusion of the self. There and only there was it possible to
live. But like Dimmesdale, she could never have her pearl without dying
for it. That is to say, the love she bore for the self in the past was a love
of the self in the future. There was no Second Coming, no truly New
World. The only way back was the way forward – a kind of evolution
in reverse in which the "supposed person" devolved into the matter she
had contemplated.

It has been said that Dickinson often leaves the poem before it is finished. With the notable exception of the 1955 variorum, most editions
lull us into the belief that the poems, though ambiguous, were literally
finished. With the publication of *The Manuscript Books* (1981) we now
know that more than a few poems contain multiple conclusions – alternative lines that tag along with the poem. This facsimile edition of poems
Dickinson made into "books" also reminds us of how tentative many of
the poems were, with lines crowding the margins of the fascicle sheets.
The poems are unfinished because they are reflections of the life that is
never "finished" until it is over. She left the poems before they were
finished just as she had to leave the life before it was finished. The finished poem was as much a contradiction as the finished life. Nothing
mattered after the life was over (as far as the present self was concerned).
Everything that ever mattered had to be in the middle. Obviously, one

---

*My reading of this poem is influenced by Paul Christensen's unpublished interpretation.

of the reasons Dickinson never willingly published any of her poems was that the printed version would have been "finished" and thus no longer her psychological property. (See, for example, her response to the publication of "The Snake" in 1866.) Just as no great poem ever "resolves" anything, the manuscript versions of her poems (and the only versions the author touched) often could not resolve even the choice of lines. It might be said that the manuscript poems belong to Emily Dickinson, and the printed poems belong to us as readers. Just as many of the manuscript poems left Dickinson with a choice, the printed versions leave us with a choice. That is to say, in both cases we find ourselves in the middle of something. It is indeed a disservice to say that Dickinson wrote about death most of the time, because the fact is that she wrote instead always about life. Death was the end, and this poet was always in the middle. She selected her own society, which was the self, and proceeded to measure it against the past from which it was supposed to have emerged. That was the "supposed person," and this was the "real person." The "supposed person" was somehow much better, the "real person" somehow a vagrant "on the town." The "real person" was a pauper with nothing to save and nothing to spend. He always found himself lost in the middle, but unlike Edwin Arlington Robinson's Miniver Cheevy he loved it, because, as Henry James has taught us, the real thing was never the same thing. Only the past and the future remained unchanged and untouched. The present was nothing but change. "I find ecstasy in living," we will recall Dickinson telling Higginson in 1870; "the mere sense of living is joy enough." Of course, James knew what Dickinson knew: that reality is in the mind and not in the matter, which never really changes. Reality was the way inward, and thus Dickinson selected her own society.

That society was the isolation we all encounter *in medias res*. Life was isolation from its beginning: "The first Day that I was a Life" was shrouded in secrecy. We were not God's children exactly, but at best His godchildren. Like Hawthorne's Pearl, we could not recognize our parents – locate our source – until the Original Sin of our being had been expiated. Death had to occur before there could be life. In *The Scarlet Letter* Dimmesdale has to die before Pearl can live a "normal" life. In our fiction life was possible only after a similar "death." That is to say, we never really lived or understood the concept of "success" until we embraced the meaning of death. It was as if we had to die out of the old life in order to experience the new or real one. We had to lose the life of society in order to gain "the mere sense of living." It was "joy enough." Any*more* was the fiction that made the life meaningful in the first place. The ways in which death defined life were legion, and Dickinson – as a kind of inverted Elizabeth Barrett Browning – never stopped counting the ways.

Naturally, the Amherst poet was only mildly interested in the author of *Sonnets from the Portuguese*. Barrett-Browning was held up to her by J. G. Holland, T. W. Higginson, and others as a literary model. Holland, editor of *Scribner's Magazine*, even sent Dickinson a picture of the English poet's tomb. She promptly gave it to Higginson, Holland's compatriot in the campaign for an American literature that was naïve instead of native. (They both objected strenuously to Whitman's book.) In her most famous sonnet Barrett-Browning concludes, "I shall but love thee better after death." For Dickinson, however, the picture was the greater reality and the greater possibility. And her giving it to Higginson in 1870 was both an ironic and a sardonic gesture. That year she told him, "Enough is so vast a sweetness I suppose it never occurs – only pathetic counterfeits – Fabulous to me as the men of the Revelations who 'shall not hunger any more.'" Dickinson's "Business" was with life's "pathetic counterfeits" – the illusions that Higginson thought were real. She knew that what remained of the love described in *Sonnets* was represented by the photograph. All that remained were "Those Boys and Girls, in Canvas – / Who stay upon the Wall." And this was enough for Dickinson.

Perhaps her challenge to Barrett-Browning's optimism is best expressed in J. 156, written possibly in the year of the English poet's death:

> You love me – you are sure –
> I shall not fear mistake –
> I shall not *cheated* wake –
> Some grinning morn –
> To find the Sunrise left –
> And Orchards – unbereft –
> And Dollie – gone!

The rest of the poem serves as a refrain for the idea that it is better not to trust the beginning of anything. In "You Love Me – You Are Sure" the protagonist treats this new love as if it were already in the middle – that is, with its passion already spent. Experience required that we would always *"cheated"* wake" – with the particular love somehow dissolved into the general. Mocked by "Some grinning morn" with its beautiful sunrise and "unbereft" orchards, we found ourselves in the middle with Dimmesdale. We will recall that the minister, his heart quickened by the meeting with Hester, returns from the wood determined to turn the clock back to the beginning of his love affair. Following their passionate reunion and determination to flee back to the Old World, however, he finds himself strangely in the middle of the life that drove him into the Dark Wood in the first place. Nothing has changed but his perspective. The townspeople "looked neither older nor younger, now; the beards of the aged were no whiter, nor could the creeping babe of yesterday walk on his feet to-day; it was impossible to describe in what respect they differed from the individuals on whom he had so recently bestowed a parting glance; and yet the minister's deepest sense seemed to inform him of their mutability." We are told that the "intervening space of a single day had operated on his consciousness like the lapse of years." Dimmesdale emerges from the forest to discover the same truth that Dickinson discovered on the second story: that life is a maze whose beginning is as inscrutable as its end. Only the middle with its subtle mutability is available to us. And, indeed, it is the reason for my shift into the present tense here, for at the end of something, we always find that life has left us in the middle or present – and never in the uroboric past.

Chapter 6

THE MASTER'S HOUSE

It has been asked recently whether Emily Dickinson ever "married," but perhaps a more helpful question is whether the poet ever attempted or at least considered suicide. Already married to herself for better or worse, she may have decided at one point or another on the ultimate divorce, that final act that tears the mind from its matter. Clearly, the most trying time in her life (for reasons still unclear) was in the early months of 1862. This was the year of her third "Master" letter, in which she described herself as having "a Tomahawk" in her side. Further evidence of an emotional struggle that year comes from a letter to her by the Rev. Charles Wadsworth. "I am distressed beyond measure at your note, received this moment," he wrote. "I can only imagine the affliction which has befallen, or is now befalling you." It appears, however, that the crisis did not involve Wadsworth directly, for though he was understandably anxious to learn more about the source of her distress, he also admitted to having "no right to intrude upon your sorrow." Dickinson may have threatened suicide obliquely, yet clearly enough to elicit Wadsworth's concern, even fear for her safety.

We will probably never know the details of the poet's relationship with the Philadelphia clergyman, whose pulpit fame in America was second only to that of Henry Ward Beecher of Brooklyn. Her first encounter with him in 1855 on her return from Washington, D.C., and the subsequent meetings have been discussed by practically everyone who has written on Dickinson, and still not much is known. We do know that the two resembled each other in their antisocial personalities. Dickinson was "public," one might say, only in the fact that she wrote poetry. Wadsworth was public only in his dedication to preaching; the clergyman generally refused to greet his congregation after services and avoided casual relationships altogether. Richard B. Sewall suggests that Emily found "a fellow sufferer" in Wadsworth. Whatever the case, the poet's note to the Philadelphian marks the first time she went beyond her "Father's ground" for help. Later that year she would leave the house again, in her letters to Thomas Wentworth Higginson. It appears that by the spring of 1862 Dickinson was ready to write her letter to the external world. Having written the bulk (and the best) of her poetry, she now felt the urgent need to go beyond the family portals for inspiration. The associations she formed have already been touched upon (and will be once again in the concluding chapter), but the question before us now concerns the importance of the Homestead on Main Street to Dickinson's evolution as an artist. By 1862 she must have realized where and how far its ancestral corridors had brought her. How the mansion brought Dickinson to herself and also to the brink of suicide is the concern of this chapter.

There in her father's house, built by her grandfather in 1814, she had conducted the great correspondence with herself. These were the poems, letters all addressed to the world of the self. It was a world within the world peopled by her family and threatened at times by visitors, both announced and unannounced. Yet the poet was generally safe from either internal or external intrusions. On his visit to the Dickinson mansion in 1870, Higginson described it as a place "where each member runs his or her own selves." And whenever neighbors approached, there was at least one escape route to the bedroom on the second story. Floor plans for the house before its 1916 renovation by the Parke family indicate the existence of backstairs off the pantry. These were known to the Dickinsons as the "Northwest Passage" – Emily's shortcut from the kitchen to her room on the southwest corner of the house. There she could shut the door on the world of everything but herself. It is safe to say, in fact, that she wrote poetry nowhere but in that room throughout her life.

The following poem has been perhaps interpreted too literally, as a description of how she receives a letter from a secret lover or otherwise confidential correspondent:

> The Way I read a Letter's – this –
> 'Tis first – I lock the Door –
> And push it with my fingers – next –
> For transport it be sure –
>
> And then I go the furthest off
> To counteract a knock –
> Then draw my little letter forth
> And slowly pick the lock –
>
> Then – glancing narrow, at the Wall –
> And narrow at the floor

> For firm Conviction of a Mouse
> Not exorcised before –
>
> Peruse how infinite I am
> To no one that You – know
> And sigh for lack of Heaven – but not
> The Heaven God bestow –   (J. 636)

The poem is not about the receipt of a lover's missive but about the isolation necessary for the most serious kind of introspection. What Dickinson keeps out of the room is as important as what she conceals there. The poem is about the delicate balance between society and the self, between all animal life (even "a Mouse") and the ego that strives to transcend animal or human limitations. This ultimate state of privacy is necessary to get beyond society's naïve illusions about existence, its insistence upon a social self that discouraged the kind of egotism she celebrated in her poems. The house kept out the neighbors, but the room excluded the more serious threat to the artist. The family members were the internal selves of society – that consanguineous extension that posed an even greater threat to the force of the central self.

Concealed within the ancestral house, she slowly picked the lock to her own artistic consciousness. Play on the phrase "picking the lock" suggests the surreptitious entry into the private room of the self, almost masturbatory in its imagery to suggest that the artist's psyche is stimulated only and always in absolute privacy. Here she read (and wrote) the letters to the world of herself and nobody else – no dead or even imaginary lover but the self destined for biological death, the self indeed already dead to the illusions about love and any *particular* life after death.

What was not dead, she proved with every poem, was her vision of infinity in the finite present. In spite of the impermanence of home and hearth, flesh and blood, she certified her existence in the language of art and its grasp upon being. This is the import of the letters and poems she wrote to herself in that corner room of the psyche. In other parts of the house, and in the world at large, one might "sigh" for the heaven that God traditionally withheld from man in this life. Yet her "perusal" was directed at this world, where body and soul do not correspond. Indeed, her poetry, like all great art, found its source and animus in the lack of correspondence between the self's version and vision. Whitman, her counterpart in American poetry, sought to restore the balance between body and soul. Dickinson thrived upon the contradiction. Whereas Whitman resorted to the exhibitionism of the "barbaric yawp" in his insistence on the equality of body and soul, Dickinson quietly retreated to her second-story bedroom in the Master's House. She would not find

God so democratically – "in the faces of men and women" – but only in the ancestry of father, grandfather, and ultimately godfather. God came to her as "a stern Preceptor" whose lesson taught her the true meaning of "Success."

Readers preferring to see Dickinson as hopelessly pining after a lover instead of her beginning in the unconscious are forced to read the poetry piecemeal. One recent study, for example, offers only the first stanza of J. 418 as evidence of the poet's "secret sorrow":

> Not in this World to see his face –
> Sounds long – until I read the place
> Where this – is said to be
> But just the Primer – to a life –
> Unopened – rare – Upon the Shelf –
> Clasped yet – to Him – and me –

"Those who would see Dickinson's lover as God or Christ, and the love poems as those of a mystic," the argument continues, "must run aground on such poems as this." But the second stanza suggests that even such sentimental readers as Mabel Loomis Todd and Higginson (who as her editors entitled the poem "The First Lesson") were more perceptive. The second and final stanza makes it clear that the rewards of the next world – even the possession of a distant lover – simply will not satisfy the demands and needs of the self in the finite or selfless present. In fact, such deferred dreams trick the self out of its artistic chamber and into the corridors of the ancestral funhouse. Although she says in the first stanza of J. 418 that such hopes of heavenly fulfillment are a "Primer" to a "life / Unopened – rare – [and] Upon the Shelf," in the next stanza she brings us down with the kind of realism that characterizes most of her important poems:

> And yet – My Primer suits me so
> I would not choose – a Book to know
> Than that – be sweeter wise –
> Might some one else – so learned – be –
> And leave me – just my A–B–C–
> Himself – could have the Skies –

To say that a poet as important as Emily Dickinson would allow herself to live in the "next world" – or *for* it – is to suggest a caricature that approaches the satire of Mark Twain's Emmeline Grangerford, who at the death of a neighbor was always on hand with her "tribute" immediately following the doctor and almost always before the undertaker. Dickinson beats both the doctor and the undertaker, of course, in her insistence that the primer to life *was* life, that others could have "the

Skies" as long as she was left with the ABCs of life. Life was always *in medias res* and never in the vicinity of the Edenic beginning or the happy ending of the Christian's Promised Land. In other words, one could not defer life in the Master's House. He could not dwell quietly in its parlor, waiting for his hopes to be granted from the second story. He was forced instead to roam its haunted family corridors until he found that secret staircase to the second story of himself. The idea of waiting below for answers instead of searching (even in vain) for them was a denial of one's existence in the here and now. It is appropriately parodied in "I Shall Know Why – When Time Is Over" (J. 193). After the poet has "ceased to wonder why,"

> Christ will explain each separate anguish
> In the fair schoolroom in the sky –

The schoolboy imagery mocks the notion that life is a waiting room, mocks the idea that death is somehow a life worth *waiting* for. Life was a search for the self in the Master's House. One either sought out that second-story version of himself or lost himself in the external world of Christian platitudes and sentimental visions of a second mortgage.

In fact, the mortgage on the Amherst house on Main Street had already been foreclosed once. By 1833 Samuel Fowler Dickinson in his dream to make Amherst College financially solvent had overextended himself, and the Homestead was sold to General David Mack, Jr., of Middlefield, Massachusetts. The first "master" of the house, so to speak, had been forced into the street; he went out West in poor spirits and died soon after. The second "master," Emily's father, could not get the house back until 1855, upon Mack's death. "My father only reads on Sunday," the poet told Higginson in 1870; "he reads *lonely & rigorous* books." In the rigorous post-Puritan New England (still more rigorous in the Connecticut Valley), Sunday was a day for introspection and spiritual concern, the first day of the week. We can imagine the master of the Homestead occupying the downstairs library and staring into one of those *"lonely & rigorous* books." Emily might be reading her own book in her room; or she might be in the kitchen, located in the rear wing of the house, beyond the pantry and diningroom. There with Vinnie and perhaps her mother (if not upstairs – but never on the "second story" – in bed, acting out her identity crisis as a woman in Victorian America) the poet would have rejoined the family, those other selves who roamed the empty corridors of love and marriage instead of those of love and death. They kept approaching but never quite careering into the trick mirrors that led one down the hall to nowhere – and nobody. They never found their Northwest Passages.

Squire Dickinson, at least, looked for his but, as a proper post-Calvin-ist, only on Sundays. What he found in the room of himself, however, was not the infinity of the self his daughter had discovered but a room lined with *"lonely & rigorous* books," thoughts from the eternal past. "Let us prepare for a life of rational happiness," he had told Emily Norcross Dickinson during their courtship in the 1820s, one of "industry, frugal-ity, [and] application." But for most of their marriage the forecast proved to be grimmer than the actuality. Dickinson, who had been graduated near the top of his class at Yale, became a lawyer and treasurer of Am-herst College (for thirty-seven years). He participated in a life of public affairs that culminated with his election to the United States House of Representatives. By the 1870s, however, he was (as Emily described him) back in the Homestead library, reading the books of those who addressed an "Eclipse" instead of themselves. Edward Dickinson's isolation dif-fered from his daughter's in that he read letters *from* the world instead of letters he might have written to the world of himself. His letters were always from the "first-story" library and never from the "second-story" bedroom of the soul who selected its own society.

That society was never to be found on Sunday, the worst day for such letter writing and reading:

> I never felt at Home – Below –
> And in the Handsome Skies
> I shall not feel at Home – I know –
> I dont like Paradise –
>
> Because it's Sunday – all the time –
> And Recess – never comes –
> And Eden'll be so lonesome
> Bright Wednesday Afternoons –
>
> If God could make a visit –
> Or ever took a Nap –
> So not to see us – but they say
> Himself – a Telescope
>
> Perennial beholds us –
> Myself would run away
> From Him – and Holy Ghost – and All –
> But there's the "Judgment Day"!   (J. 413)

Below in the library of the Master's House, it was Sunday "all the time." There with its promises of "paradise" in the next life, the poet could never feel at home. "Recess" never came there.

On Sundays, and for months and months of Sundays until "all the time had leaked" (J. 322), one meekly applied for that second mortgage on life. Instead of risking the loss of the house by ignoring the external world of lawyers and bankers, one borrowed on his spiritual resources. He borrowed and borrowed, begged and borrowed for his very life until there was no life to care about:

> When we have ceased to care
> The Gift is given
> For which we gave the Earth
> And mortgaged Heaven
> But so declined in worth
> T'is ignominy now
> To look upon –   (J. 1706)

Unlike her father and grandfather, Dickinson refused to accept a second mortgage from the godfather of them all. Edward Dickinson had lived the lawyer's truth, and Samuel Fowler Dickinson had lived the banker's truth (in his attempt to acquire "second mortgages" for Amherst College). They had both mortgaged the house of God the Father, given up their "infinity" in the present, in order to pay for the house on Main Street. Their "Northwest Passage" led nowhere but out the front door and into the law offices and financial institutions – right into the world that dissolved the society of the central self. It was always a world of the future, where payments had to be made on time. And its result was finally ignominy "To look upon."

Dickinson might have said "looked *down* upon," for she seldom descended from the second story for anything but family banter – with a father who cared only for her bread, a mother who did "not care for thought," and a sister who dwelled interminably on the quotidian level, or first story. "Two Editors of Journals came to my Father's House, this winter – and asked me for my Mind," she bragged to Higginson in 1862. When she asked them why, "they said . . . they, would use it for the World." Like her father and grandfather, the editors were the first-story types, probably Samuel Bowles and Josiah P. Holland. They would have found anything from the "Northwest Passage" unconventional at best. Bowles, of course, was far more tolerant as an editor than Holland (who once returned a poem of Whitman's with an insulting note), and he had once persuaded the poet to see him when she refused to descend for any other external visitors. She refused these editors because they would publish only garbled versions of her work – poems that rhymed, parsed, and spelled right, poems that above all made sense. Generally, the literary world of her day were kept waiting endlessly in the parlor.

They finally had to settle for what they thought they perceived to be literature: the sentimentality and banality of the "scribbling women" who dominated the literary journals of Dickinson's day. These were outside both house and garden (today inside *Better Homes and Gardens*). Such works did not look for the serpent in the House or the ghoul in the Garden. It was either, on the one hand, the "faction" of Helen Hunt Jackson and her Indians or, on the other, the fiction of Harriet Prescott Spofford's "Circumstance" (about nothing truly circumstantial). Dickinson knew that the serpent now dwelled in the Master's House and was no longer consigned to the Eden of earthly illusions. It had left the Garden, now haunted by the ghoulish corpses of the human condition, and moved into the House that housed the psyche of the artist. It had followed Dickinson up her "Northwest Passage" to make the Fall of Man a fall into identity instead of annonymity. It was a "narrow Fellow," indeed, that got between dreamers and their dream of a New Eden or a Happy Ending. The serpent was now a strange power in the corner room of the corner room of the psyche.

In perhaps a veiled complaint about the worn-out illusions that preoccupied most writers of current fiction, Dickinson told Higginson, "When much in the Woods as a little Girl, I was told that the Snake would bite me, that I might pick a poisonous flower, or Goblins kidnap me, but I went along and met no one but Angels. . . . so I hav'nt that confidence in fraud which many exercise." This was the fraud that could not "cheat the Bee" (J. 130). Likewise, this poet was not to be tricked – as were many of her literary contemporaries – by the Indian summer of a Second Coming or New Eden. The Garden no longer held the serpent or its original inhabitants. It had left the Garden and pursued the Adam and Eve of our psyche into the Master's House – that place where Dickinson was always threatened with becoming "Mrs. Adam" instead of Eve. April was "the cruellest month" in the nineteenth century as well as in the twentieth, for the corpse of the human condition could not be buried in the Garden. It reappeared in the House as "A snake with mottles rare":

> Surveyed my chamber floor
> In feature as the worm before
> But ringed with power

The lines come from "In Winter in My Room" (J. 1670). The poem records a dream in which

> I came upon a Worm
> Pink lank and warm
> But as he was a worm
> And worms presume

> Not quite with him at home
> Secured him by a string
> To something neighboring
> And went along

But, as a subsequent stanza reveals, the worm evolved into the serpent:

> I shrank – "How fair you are"!
> Propitiation's claw –
> "Afraid he hissed
> Of me"?
> "No cordiality" –

With the Fall of Man, the House and Garden had become inversions of one another. In the beginning, there had been the Garden, out of which grew the cordiality of the human condition or the "hansom" man. From Emerson's benevolent nature came the serpent or corpse of that postlapsarian state that could not be buried permanently or in any way avoided. No mansion, certainly not the ancestral one of the Dickinsons, was citadel enough to keep out nature or its creeping creatures of change.

A recent critical fantasy suggests that Dickinson became pregnant (perhaps by Wadsworth) and even underwent an abortion. Although the theory is far-fetched, its value as a key to Dickinson's ontology is nevertheless useful. Indeed, we might take the idea a step further and imagine that she buried the fetus in the garden. All this is to say that the absurdity of such an incident in Dickinson's life is no greater than the absurdity of a Hester without her Pearl. As T. S. Eliot taught us in *The Waste Land*, the life we as human beings are forced to follow cannot be buried in the Garden as if it were an unwanted fetus. Ever and anon, it returns to haunt us in the Master's House. One might try to flee, but there is no possibility of the happy ending we find in Spofford's "Circumstance" (where the heroine finally escapes from the "Indian Devil"). Thus, in the final stanza of J. 1670, the flight from the serpent begins and ends in the Master's House:

> That time I flew
> Both eyes his way
> Lest he pursue
> Nor ever ceased to run
> Till in a distant Town
> Towns on from mine
> I set me down
> This was a dream –

One might enjoy the fantasy, but he always woke up back home with the human condition.

Indeed, the human condition was the "home" condition. Emerson may have urged that man was "at home" where he found himself – "in markets, in senates, in battles." Dickinson's spiritual agoraphobia, on the other hand, taught her that man was "at home" only in the Master's House of his fears about his own mortality. Such Emersonian traveling was merely "a fool's paradise." This is the difference between the "Manifest Destiny" of Emerson's American Renaissance and the brutal awakening of Dickinson's America during the Civil War. Her American poet was "at home" now only behind the locked door, beneath the wax that sealed the letter to himself. Dickinson probed the "Northwest Passage" of herself, while Emerson looked again "in vain" for the poet he had once described and Whitman searched for a "passage to more than India." Nothing was "manifest" now except the self without a destiny:

> Those – dying then,
> Knew where they went –
> They went to God's Right Hand
> That Hand is amputated now
> And God cannot be found –

Of course, the second stanza warns that such nihilism makes human behavior "small" – that

> Better an ignis fatuus
> Than no illume at all –   (J. 1551)

The qualification is not an argument for Emersonian self-reliance but one for the *ignis fatuus* of the brooding self, that flickering illusive flame at the end of the tunnel that insists that whatever the character of the soul its destiny is achieved in the present. As she told Higginson, "the mere sense" of living was enough. It was better, therefore, to remain in the Master's House and not exhaust one's energy on the one next door. The mansion had slipped away from the family once before. The Dickinsons had been forced into domestic exile on Pleasant Street. But Pleasant Street had not been Main Street, and their home there had not been the Homestead.

One had to roam the ancestral home of himself in order to find the self that really mattered. Dickinson learned this lesson all too well by the time she wrote her frantic letter to Wadsworth in 1862. His answer (and we surely lack much of his correspondence to her) may have saved her life. Since many of her letters are also missing (burned by Vinnie), we have no way of knowing the nature of her response to his advice. He may have recommended psychological counseling; for all we know, the eye treatment in Boston in 1864 and 1865 may have been for the other "I" as well. Something – or someone – saved her life. For reasons still to be unraveled, the Master's House had become a death house, a "Cornice – in the Ground" – to the artistic spirit. Dickinson needed help from the outside. This may have come from Higginson. In recalling their initial correspondence she told him in 1869, "You were not aware that you saved my Life." By this time, however, she had reconciled herself to the domestic (and artistic) prison and could refuse Higginson's repeated invitations to forsake the House for visits to the Boston literati for their weekly meetings. In fact, she could tell her Norcross cousins about the same time, "I am in bed to-day – a curious place for me." She added that she could not write there as well (any longer?), "but [could] love as well, and long more."

But back in the early 1860s, loving must have been more on the side of longing. There are more than a few poems, some sent to friends, that critics have classified as suicidal. In her letter to Wadsworth, Dickinson may have enclosed the following:

> What if I say I shall not wait!
> What if I burst the fleshly Gate –
> And pass escaped – to thee
>
> What if I file this Mortal – off –
> See where it hurt me – That's enough –
> And step in Liberty!
>
> They cannot take me – any more!
> Dungeons can call – and Guns implore
> Unmeaning – now – to me
>
> As laughter – was – an hour ago –
> Or Laces – or a Travelling Show –
> Or who died – yesterday!   (J. 277)

The addressee of this poem (if not God Himself) may be dead, but of course Wadsworth could be the addressee in the sense of geography, that distance finally deadens intimacy. In fact, most of her relationships outside the family had been hindered by geography. Ratio *was* reality in the sense that separation was necessary for a love in which the lover did not change. But it was not one person but the "supposed person" that she missed, the one who would never change and yet still defy the stasis of such an arrangement. Poetry appeared to be the only escape from such a

reality, especially in the Master's House, where "The Brain has corridors – surpassing / Material Place." Even this relief had its costs, however, for solitude became loneliness with the departure of the muse. That
is to say, Dickinson realized around 1862 (all dates are arbitrary or only
generally located with this poet) that she had come as far as she could
and that what she had really been celebrating was her own mortality. If
so, she had become in that corner room her own potential assassin –
now "hid in our Apartment":

> The Body – borrows a Revolver –
> He bolts the Door –
> O'erlooking a superior spectre –
> Or More –   (J. 670)

For a time at least Dickinson may have found in the Master's House not
"Infinity" in her room but a "Funeral" in her brain (J. 280). All of those
corridors now led to the "superior spectre" of the "hansom" man. In
that case, why not get done with the carriage ride? "Tie the Strings to
my Life," she proclaims –

> Then, I am ready to go!
> Just look at the Horses –
> Rapid! That will do!   (J. 279)

The soul had its "Bandaged moments." The middle of this poem makes
the message more explicit:

> The soul has moments of Escape –
> When bursting all the doors –
> She dances like a Bomb, abroad,
> And swings upon the Hours,   (J. 512)

In the Master's House, the one built not by her grandfather but by God
the Father and mortgaged to the godfather ever afterward, Dickinson
had been taking her own life, taking it back toward the Eden of desire
but also dangerously close to the deadly Wall of Flames that separates
consciousness from unconsciousness. As genius comes perilously close
to insanity, so the act of this poet took her close to spiritual suicide.

Singed by the experience, bandaged and "brayed of Tongue" after
those intensely creative years of "The Soul's retaken moments" (J. 512),
she was now spiritually and aesthetically exhausted, for poetry, as Emerson taught her, *had* been "written before time was." As Emerson's *other*
poet she had also heard those primal warblings. But unlike Whitman,
who heard the voice of the Elder Brother, God, she heard only the voice

of the godfather. Dickinson's poetry never transcends the guilt over experience. As a consequence, it picks up the American theme and dream where Whitman loses it in such poems as "Out of the Cradle Endlessly Rocking" and "As I Ebb'd with the Ocean of Life." Where he concludes his great American verse with the sound of "peals of distant ironical laughter" at every word he has written, Dickinson begins the song of America's (and her own) all-too-manifest destiny.

How does one live with such a theme? The dilemma, indeed crisis, Whitman faced at the close of his period of greatest poetry was the realization that such Emersonian experiments with language could uplift but not sustain man in his vision of having (as Whitman does in "Song of Myself") a first-name relationship with God the Father. One was instead a stranger in his own house, a pariah in his own village. As a poet with such a theme, Dickinson faced the challenge of her fictional counterpart in American literature. Like Hester Prynne after her release from prison, Dickinson after those "procreant" years in the Master's House was free to return to the Old World, too – that is, to the seeming peace of Amherst society.

She did not, perhaps for the same reason Hawthorne gives for Hester's decision to remain on the outskirts of the village of Boston after her release from prison: "There is a fatality . . . which almost invariably compels human beings to linger around and haunt, ghost-like, the spot where some great and marked event has given the color to their lifetime." Hawthorne tells us that Hester's "sin, her ignominy, were the roots which she had struck into the soil." Dickinson's "ignominy" had been her salvation as well. It had been her root – and her route of evanescence. She had celebrated herself on the second story, as Hester had with Dimmesdale in the forest. In the Master's House she had mastered herself. This was her ignominy: She had made the corner room the center of the house. She had refused to join her father in the library or her family in the parlor – both waiting rooms for the godfather.

In *The Scarlet Letter* when Hester "half playfully" remonstrates her illegitimate child by saying, "Thou art no Pearl of mine!" we remember that the mother's reverse psychology backfires when the child – in answer then as to whose child she really is – replies, "I have no Heavenly Father!" In the next chapter Pearl weeps inexplicably at the sight of a rose growing before the governor's mansion. Immediately afterward they both "hear voices in the garden," and the child is subjected to a religious interrogation by the governor and his minister. Hawthorne knew the value of a myth as well as Faulkner (his twentieth-century counterpart in American fiction), and so the reader of *The Scarlet Letter* has already learned that although Governor Bellingham was almost godlike in his ecclesiastical and civil powers, "the chances of a popular election had caused this

former ruler to descend a step or two from the highest rank." Hawthorne's cryptic message here is echoed in Dickinson's cryptic poetry.
With the Fall of Man, God had stepped down "from the highest rank."
No longer God of the angels or man before the Fall, He had become the
godfather in the sense of the distance he placed between Himself and His
creations. The godfather was a good father but no longer God the Father,
man's Heavenly Father. He was, however, the only "father" man knew.
He was the Dimmesdale in the forest whom man dare not approach,
even at the behest of his earthly mother.

The true and legitimate father, on the other hand, would have been as
loving as the earthly mother (or self-love). But He had become at best
the godfather, a distant "relative" – at worst the Master of the House.
When the master of the Homestead died in 1874, his son Austin is alleged
to have kissed him on the forehead, saying, "There, father, I never dared
do that while you were living." Dickinson herself was shocked at how
shocked she was at Edward Dickinson's passing. Yet she declined to join
her brother and sister at their father's deathbed and never visited his grave.
Of course, by this time the poet was habitually house bound. There is,
however, a deeper significance to her actions – or inaction. Edward
Dickinson had been the Master of the House and not, in the sense of his
emotional inaccessibility, the father of his children. The same had been
true of the Heavenly Father Pearl rightfully denies. All she had was
Dimmesdale. And all Emily Dickinson the poet had was what Higginson
described after his 1870 visit as a "thin dry & speechless" specter of a
father.

In a poem once described as "one of the most offensive bits of contemp-
tuous Unitarianism," Dickinson spoke of God the Father as "a distant –
stately Lover" who woos us "by His Son." It was a "Vicarious Courtship," she complained, in which we were invited to "Choose the Envoy – and spurn the Groom" (J. 357). In other words, the human condition invited us, tricked us, into an illicit relationship with ourselves.
Indeed, it was masturbatory in the sense that it made us both the parent
and child of our own dilemma. We were both Hester and Pearl – the
bearer and the ill-begotten but never the begetter. We never really knew
who our Father was. For Emerson Christ may have been the first man
to know his divinity, but for Dickinson Christ was the last one to know
it. For her and the rest of us, it was an "immaculate conception" – or
contraception in which God the Father came to us as the "dry & speechless" godfather. One might argue that Austin Dickinson was "the only
begotten son" in the Dickinson family, but the evidence suggests that
Edward Dickinson was no more than godfather to all of his children –
and no more than "Envoy" to his wife.

It is appropriate that the wild rosebush is our symbol for the consuming passion that makes us all the illegitimate children of God. It represents life without death, and that desire always draws forth the Voice in the Garden. Dickinson kept hearing that voice of guilt, but she never abandoned the rose. Her "supposed persons" never give up completely that part of their nature that flourishes in the most unpromising environments. The wild rosebush represents man's desire to be God – to grow without change and to love without loss – and as such it is our substitute for the Burning Bush, for God the Father never revealed Himself that directly. Instead of miracles, He sent the godfather or the lover-son – always an envoy and never Himself.

Under these circumstances, one stayed at home and made his own house the temple of God. He defied the godfather by finding God not in envoys but in himself:

> Some keep the Sabbath going to Church –
> I keep it, staying at Home –
> With a Bobolink for a Chorister –
> And an Orchard, for a Dome –
>
> Some keep the Sabbath in Surplice –
> I just wear my Wings –
> And instead of tolling the Bell, for Church,
> Our little Sexton – sings.
>
> God preaches, a noted Clergyman –
> And the sermon is never long,
> So instead of getting to Heaven, at last –
> I'm going, all along.   (J. 324)

This poem has been read as either Dickinson's playful apostasy or her transcendentalist's desire to find God in nature rather than in old books or outworn ceremonies. But the God she defies is the godfather, and the nature she celebrates is the garden of her own mind in the Master's House, for she wrote, as I have said, steadfastly before the Fall of Man – and after the fall of Emerson. In other words, she found God not "in the coarse" of nature with Emerson but in the "mind alone" on the second story. Always Eve before the advent of "Mrs. Adam," Dickinson resisted the "matter" of nature and remained back with the possibility of the "mind alone without corporeal friend."

Emerson's god, like her father's "Eclipse," shut out the self in the present. In both cases, it was "Sunday – all the time" (J. 413): the Not-Me waiting to become the Real Me. *Her* Sunday, on the other hand, let in God the Father, "a noted Clergyman" whose sermon was "never long" because there was no eclipse of the self. In the Homestead, God or the self was always being eclipsed by the godfather, the Master of the House who gave his daughter books but begged her not to read them. "He fears," she told Higginson, "they joggle the Mind." The godfather was "too busy with his Briefs – to notice what we do." In such a home – man's home – God came to her not as a loving father but as a lawyer, that individual who subscribes to a code of justice that is ultimately fraudulent because it is "blind." His sermon was "never long" either, because it was a "Brief" in its bloodless language of disinterested action. Dickinson's sermon to herself, on the other hand, was long – as long and *interested as* 1,775 poems. Really, they were all brief sermons to the self to be true to the so-called Not-Me in the present and not to the godfather's code of justice. They were all attempts to circumvent the godfather-lawyer and speak directly to our accuser, God the Father.

In this regard, her poems were always songs and never prayers, chants (or hymns) instead of direct supplications, for in her church it was High Mass all the time. The prayer with its prose was for the godfather. The chant was reserved for God the Father. It transcended the quotidian facts of the human condition and conjured up God Himself. "Let Emily sing for you because she cannot pray." Such confrontations, of course, can be considered "suicidal," likened perhaps to Ahab's hopeless quest of the White Whale in *Moby-Dick,* for Dickinson also wore white as the defiant bride of experience. She was the bridesmaid and never the bride of the lover-son-envoy – or daughter to be "given away" by the godfather. Her crisis in 1862, therefore, was the result of her willingness to stand "accused" before God and chant her innocence. To do so was to go to the brink of suicide and the edge of sanity. She risked a premature burial that year and came away from the experience as strong as Hester Prynne after her decision to live out her life in Boston. Like Hester, Dickinson found God in the Not-Me and so recovered her innocence in the present.

The letter in Hawthorne's masterpiece that denotes the guilt of the Not-Me is the first letter of the alphabet, of course. And to regain his innocence the pilgrim had to journey back before language to the unconscious myth of himself. Dickinson's poetry often does this in its ability to sound the chant of the Not-Me – that very self Emerson and others consign to oblivion. Like the haunting sound of an American Indian dance, her poems tell us something about the self before it became the Not-Me of the New World. Her poems explain with their curious cadences what they cannot explain – namely, why God is man's accuser as well as his creator. The illusive rhythm of her verse is often found in such closing lines as "I'm going, all along" (J. 324) or in the refrain of the following poem:

> I reason, Earth is short –
> And Anguish – absolute –
> And many hurt,
> But, what of that?
>
> I reason, we could die –
> The best Vitality
> Cannot excel Decay,
> But, what of that?
>
> I reason, that in Heaven –
> Somehow, it will be even –
> Some new Equation, given –
> But, what of that?   (J. 301)

She takes us through the old equation of the human condition: the discovery that the "best Vitality" leads to the worst decay. Though the poem holds out for a "new Equation," the refrain sets the tone of melancholy and bewilderment. "But, what of that?" – life, death, and immortality. It covers all three possibilities, even though she has, so far, "never lost as much but twice":

> Burglar! Banker – Father!
> I am poor once more!

Or father! grandfather – godfather! The Not-Me was always kept "a beggar / Before the door of God" (J. 49). But what of that? What of that – even if the godfather waited for us instead of God the Father?

The Master's House was therefore always a house and never a home in the Emersonian sense of being one with God wherever one found oneself. In it we were always the Not-Me of the godfather and never the Real Me of God the Father. In this context we might reread Dickinson's comment in 1875 that "home itself is far from home since my father died." In the strict sense of the biography, of course, she is lamenting the death of her father. In the broader sense, however, she is echoing her "identity-theme" – the book that she wrote over and again in her poems. Once God the Father had stepped down from a high place, man's home became a house that tried to be haunted. Her artistry was a kind of architectural psychomachia in which the self fled from the godfather, hastened up that "Northwest Passage" to the corner room. There it celebrated the Not-Me as if home were where the heart was, instead of the hearth.

Only on the second story could she act as if the Master of the House were God instead of the godfather. That is to say, she could finally get

back before the scarlet letter, the first letter of the alphabet and the first
sign of consciousness, for with language man came to conceive of himself and to hear the Voice in the Garden. Language was merely a speech
"act." It carried the poet from the quotidian self, but the flight always
ended in the fact of denial:

> Denial – is the only fact
> Perceived by the Denied –
> Whose Will – a numb significance –
> The Day the Heaven died –
>
> And all the Earth strove common round –
> Without Delight, or Beam –
> What Comfort was it Wisdom – was –
> The spoiler of Our Home?   (J. 965)

Language finally brought the poet to "The Day the Heaven died." At
that point, she felt a "Funeral" in her brain. Such wisdom became indeed
"The spoiler of Our Home." Or as she says it another way:

> And then a Plank in Reason, broke,
> And I dropped down, and down –
> And hit a World, at every plunge,
> And Finished knowing – then –

This final stanza of the famous "I Felt a Funeral in My Brain" (J. 280) is
surely Dickinson's version and vision of the Fall of Man – or God. It is
the knowledge, as Emerson finally admitted to in "Experience," "that
we exist" only in the Master's House. Dickinson's great poetry began
with this fact of denial. "A Plank in Reason, broke," and she fell from
the lawyer's truth into the poet's truth of never knowing. All she knew
then, or at her height as a poet, was that the art of language – its "Bolts
of Melody" – brought her full circle. It stunned her but did not save her.
What it did save, however, was the sense of herself in the present. The
poetry inflated the Not-Me – that fictional self that told all the truth there
was to know on earth. She may have gone full circle with her art, but
she now possessed the art, or evidence of "how infinite" she was in the
corner room of the Master's House.

   Dickinson's crisis of 1862 had little to do, therefore, with the Rev.
Wadsworth, who was simply another "Envoy" of the godfather. It had
nothing to do with love and marriage and everything to do with love
and death. It is significant that Dickinson wrote to Wadsworth the minister during her crisis and to Higginson the former minister after it. The
first heard only about the sorrow that made her an artist; the second

heard all about her artistry. With Wadsworth it was "Sunday – all the time," but with Higginson she moved on to the first day of the work week. She got past the guilt of Sunday and into the daily celebration of herself in the Not-Me, no matter the cost. With such poetry the god-father was no longer the Master of the House.

Chapter 7

THE LEAF-FRINGED LEGEND
OF EMILY DICKINSON

It might be said of our poet on the second story what has often been said of the English poet George Herbert: that she wrote her poems straight to God and then to anyone else who cared to listen. This accounts for much of her obscurity. Her poems read like overheard conversations. We eavesdrop on a dialogue that seemingly has little to do with us. We stand back from her riddles as Keats did from the scene carved on the urn and ask the question that is itself the answer. Her "unheard melodies" ring in our ears. Of course, the poems have everything to do with us, for they ask the ultimate question of "What is?" Why do we find ourselves wedged between body and soul in the "Cold Pastoral" of the present? What "leaf-fringed legend" haunts about the shape of our existence?

We want fuller meanings from her poems, but unlike Whitman she makes us no promises. "Have you felt so proud to get at the meanings of poems?" he asks in his most promising poem. "Stop this day and night with me and you shall possess the origin of all poems." That origin is "nature without check," the source of Dickinson's poems as well. She does not, however, allow us to rest in its harmony but rather pushes us relentlessly toward its paradox. We find not Whitman's "camerado" but a deep silence that "dost tease us out of thought." She calls that silence the "Crash without a Sound." That is to say, we never see and hardly ever hear. At best we get our answer in the echo of our question – in "Life's reverberation / It's Explanation found" (J. 1581). The idea begins to crystallize when we take these lines back to the beginning of the poem:

> The farthest Thunder that I heard
> Was nearer than the Sky
> And rumbles still, though torrid Noons
> Have lain their missiles by –
> The Lightning that preceded it

> Struck no one but myself –
> But I would not exchange the Bolt
> For all the rest of Life –

Struck by "Bolts of Melody," Emily Dickinson sings not of the New World or body but of the "mind alone" that is fated to ponder the paradox of its existence.

It is the bittersweet music of thought she hears as the meanings reverberate around her. Her poems neither celebrate the world nor confess to its silence; rather, they wait out (and write out of) nature to the edge of doom. She followed her stoical New England nature into the abyss of life's contradictions and survived to tell us (and herself) about the adventure. Her more sober reports are naturally more frequent in the later poetry, after the crisis of the early 1860s. In J. 1417, for example, she is confident that her odes to experience take her to the brink of truth and no farther. Any closer, the experienced virgin knows, and the game is over:

> How Human Nature dotes
> On what it cant detect
> The moment that a Plot is plumbed
> It's meaning is extinct –
>
> Prospective is the friend
> Reserved for us to know
> When Constancy is clarified
> Of Curiosity –
>
> Of subjects that resist
> Redoubtablest is this
> Where go we –
> Go we anywhere
> Creation after this?

Had Dickinson lost her perspective or "slant" on the world, she would have no doubt preceded Camille Claudel into the lunatic asylum. She came close, and not only in the 1860s. A few years after writing this poem she lost her "closest earthly friend" in the death of Wadsworth. In 1883 she suffered what her doctor described as "nervous prostration" after the death of young Gilbert, her nephew. She survived, though weakened by the successive losses, until 1886. She did so because she kept writing about the ratio between life and death. Unlike Claudel, she never wrote her "Destiny." She never went beyond the paradox of life's "Cold Pastoral" – never took Austin's oath of "Rubicon."

In reading through her poems today, one is struck (really astounded) by her patience. She saw so much (or so *little*) from her second-story window, yet did not give in to its illusions (as Whitman's twenty-ninth bather does and indeed Whitman himself finally did). In Dickinson's poetry the god never quite flies away. He is always leaving but never departed. In the city where *Le Dieu envolé* was sculpted (and where I now write) there exists an order of individuals who exemplify in their pitiful way the patience of this poet. They are the street people, the numerous vagrants and "little tipplers" of Paris, who wait out their lives on street corners and park benches. Like George Orwell before he became Orwell, they are – as the title of his first book puts it – *Down and Out in Paris and London* and, symbolically, wherever the human condition is more complicated than that found in Orwell's most famous book, *1984*. Back in 1884 life and love for Orwell's Julia and Winston Smith would have been more difficult and bewildering. Freed of their totalitarian prison, they would have found themselves in Dickinson's "magic Prison" (J. 1601), waiting for the end of the story.

Dickinson sat down to wait, too, but on the second story. Like the beggars on the Left Bank and elsewhere, her poetry is finally a mute protest against the way of the world – against the fact that death is man's lot and so the subject of his life. "Twice have I stood a beggar / Before the door of God!" she declared. The first time the illusion of fulfillment made the waiting as easy as a carriage ride. The second time, however, is the last time; and the passenger knows all too well where the horses are headed. The only thing that mattered, therefore, was the waiting, for it was everything and the only thing clearly visible. The waiting became the writing – that continuum of thought pressed into the book that is never finished. It is little wonder she gave up her bookmaking on the second story. The fascicles are incomplete because Dickinson realized that to finish them would be to finish off her "lexicon" – the only companion she had in the search for beauty without truth.

Her decision not to bind her holographs, much less allow them to be published as complete works, also accounts for the fact that the body of her work is more or less phaseless. The "wait" goes on throughout her life and work. Other writers such as Emerson and Whitman have definable periods of optimism and pessimism, but Dickinson is never clearly a yea-sayer or a nay-sayer. She may have lived (as in fact she did) on Main Street, but she never traveled it – as did Emerson on the lecture circuit and Whitman atop an omnibus. For her such "books" or phases were "for the scholars' idle times." When she could read her own brooding nature so directly, there was never time enough to stop to put it into a book. With different phases we had at least the illusion of progress, but for Dickinson the fact remained that we were always in the middle of the same life. Whenever we forgot that truth, we were reminded of it through the immediacy of language. Our words told us that we were always *about to be* in the present – were always waiting for something.

Throughout her poems Dickinson insists that waiting is the nature of experience. We wait for what will – or will not – come. Either way it is the end of the "corporeal friend." We simply do not know when, and this is our protection. As she tells us, life consists of being blindly in the middle:

> We knew not that we were to live –
> Nor when – we are to die –
> Our ignorance – our cuirass is –
> We wear Mortality
> As lightly as an Option Gown
> Till asked to take it off –
> By his intrusion, God is known –
> It is the same with Life –   (J. 1462)

The tense shift between the first two lines is an example of the power of language. It startles us into the awareness that we are still perilously alive in the present, after allowing in the first line the objective distance possible only in our focus upon the unchangeable past. Yet as the poem proceeds we recover from the shock of the second line and become able to step outside the conditions of our mortality. This is Dickinson's version of Keats's "Negative Capability." The "corporeal friend" has no particular identity but wears what it has "As lightly as an Option Gown / Till asked to take it off." In the "mind alone" we unlock ourselves from the mirror image whose mortality has haunted us for almost a lifetime. First in infancy we came to suppose ourselves a person instead of simply an organ that took in food and motherly attention. Then in our adulthood we came to doubt that supposition and fear our mortality. The "mind alone," as we recall from Dickinson's letter to Higginson, was the letter "without corporeal friend." It was that second-story look at the self – the lie that told the truth about the "supposed person." Only through such a disembodied voice as Dickinson's could this paradox of the present be so cleverly articulated. She had indeed the art to stun herself (J. 505).

As suggested in the preceding chapter, Dickinson worked through the alienation of being mortal in her crisis years of the 1860s. God was no longer the godfather but God the Father. She was content to wait Him out. Indeed, it was an act of poetry to do so. The second story was the first step toward knowing without understanding. Emily Dickinson, as it were, returned to the Old World of myth. She no longer dwelled in the world of the New Canaan, where the first day of the week was Sunday (in no way a *bon jour*). The Old World truly rested on Sunday, but in the New it was a day on which one wrestled with his puritan conscience. He had always to ask for a second chance – indeed, for a "Second Coming." But for Dickinson the second story of the "mind alone" was enough. This was one of the reasons she could finally go outside (or downstairs) with her poetry. She could show it to Higginson because the major crisis of her life was over. She accepted the sacrifice because she was free of its guilt. Indeed, her smugness can be compared to Thoreau's placidity in the face of annihilation. Her 1870 interview with Higginson reminds us in part of the string of aphorisms at the end of Emerson's "Thoreau." Two examples will suffice:

Dickinson: Women talk: men are silent: that is why I dread women.
  Thoreau: Fire is the most tolerable third party.

Dickinson: How do most people live without any thoughts [?] . . . How do they get strength to put on their clothes in the morning [?]
  Thoreau: How can we expect a harvest of thought who have not had a seedtime of character?

Of course, Emerson was accused by Sophia Thoreau of exaggerating her brother's tendency toward coldness in human relations. No doubt it was an exaggeration, but one for which Thoreau and not Emerson was responsible. The same is true for Dickinson. In other words, to accept annihilation objectively is to exaggerate the power of the "mind alone." In what may well be an exaggeration, Thoreau is alleged to have said on his deathbed in response to the question of whether he had made his peace with God: "I did not know we had quarreled, Aunt." Such detachment from a world (and a god) that often appears so unjust is more than most of us can manage. Nor could Dickinson or Thoreau manage it entirely. That is to say, the capability to write oneself into the "mind alone" – to retreat from the cares of the "corporeal friend" – was a *negative* capability. Not only does one negate the mirror image by removing himself from it; he also removes the reason for writing in the first place. Writing is the ultimate exaggeration – that cosmic tall tale that has to close with the same narrator who began it. Thoreau might avoid for a time the problems of making a living by going off to Walden Pond, but eventually he had to follow the railroad tracks back to Concord. For the same reasons Dickinson had to descend occasionally from her second story. Without the "corporeal" world or body all we had were rumors of the soul, and that was no way to *make a living*. The life had to be made or found in the ratio between the mind and the Me:

> This Me – that walks and works – must die,
> Some fair or stormy Day,
> Adversity if it may be
> Or wild prosperity
> The Rumor's Gate was shut so tight
> Before my mind was born
> Not even a Prognostic's push
> Can make a Dent thereon –   (J. 1588)

The poem resembles Frost's "Fire and Ice" in its negative capability:

> Some say the world will end in fire,
> Some say in ice.
> From what I've tasted of desire
> I hold with those who favor fire.
> But if it had to perish twice,
> I think I know enough of hate
> To say that for destruction ice
> Is also great
> And would suffice.

In both poems the inevitable destruction of the "corporeal friend" is calmly accepted. However, Frost eventually destroys his objectivity in that although he cares little how we perish, he still wonders why. Dickinson's wall of stoicism caves in as well. She may be so far removed from the drama that she fails to care whether death will bring "Adversity" or "Wild Prosperity," but the fact that she writes at all is revealing; for it was not death but life that drew her in, and her poems suggest that it does not perish in either love or hate but is locked into a "Cold Pastoral" long before the end comes. This was Dickinson's lifelong topic. The "hansom" man is always coming but never arriving in her world. The poem is always being written but never finished for the printer. Her brother Austin may have declared his "Rubicon" with Mabel, but he was always being *called back* to his existence as Squire Dickinson. He was, as his sister knew, always *in medias res*. Frost was right, of course, to see love as one of the principal agents of destruction. Its fire "froze" us into our "Cold Pastoral"; it made us both lifeless and deathless. Like the young woman in *Le Dieu envolé*, the lovers in Keats's "Ode," or the aroused persona in "Wild Nights – Wild Nights!" we were always waiting with hands outstretched, living and dying for our pastoral experience.

The girl "with *curling hair*" grew up to become the iron maiden of

desire, her poetry, as it were, the "foster-child of silence and slow time."
As we look back upon her life and work, we have to ask what "legend"
lies behind her disembodied voice. She flees into the silence that is the
end of every great modern poem. Beginning with valentine's poems, she
grew up to write odes to experience. Between "If Recollecting Were
Forgetting" (J. 33) and "Because I Could Not Stop for Death" (J. 712)
we have the theme of love and death's dance of the macabre. The harmony of nature begins with a valentine's visit and ends with a carriage
ride toward eternity, but it is the eternity of the present. Life's acme was
to be found, she knew, in the balance between living and dying. Such a
scene is suggested in another of Claudel's sculptures, "Abandon." It shows
two lovers lost in each other's arms – the male kneeling before his lover,
who looks skyward as she is caressed and kissed. They have abandoned
their quotidian existence and are about to be born again in their sexual
union (as if the first sexual union that led to their conception had been
somehow defective). They are mortals about to become gods, but their
deification is possible nowhere but in the "mind alone."

In a poem entitled "Dying" in the 1890 edition, we find the same
balance. The personal signs of death are contrasted with the general ones
of life:

> The Sun kept setting – setting – still
> No Hue of Afternoon –
> Upon the Village I perceived –
> From House to House 'twas Noon –
>
> The Dusk kept dropping – dropping – still
> No Dew upon the Grass –
> But only on my Forehead stopped –
> And wandered in my Face –
>
> My feet kept drowsing – drowsing – still
> My fingers were awake –
> Yet why so little sound – Myself
> Unto my Seeming – make?
>
> How well I knew the Light before –
> I could not see it now –
> 'Tis Dying – I am doing – but
> I'm not afraid to know –   (J. 692)

It is the juxtaposition of life and death, the two ultimate lovers in every
pastoral experience. Or beauty and truth – much in the attitude of Claudel's lovers, the one dies into the arms of the other. The sun of one sets
in the noon of the other. Our "light" fails in broad daylight.

This account of Emily Dickinson opened with the story of Austin Dickinson's declaration of "Rubicon" in his love affair with the woman who
became the poet's first editor. The act was clearly Emersonian in that it
reminds us of a similar declaration in "Self-Reliance," something Austin
might have told his wife:

> I must be myself. I cannot break myself any longer for you. . . . If
> you can love me for what I am, we shall be the happier. If you
> cannot, I will still seek to deserve that you should. I will not hide
> my tastes or aversions. I will so trust that what is deep is holy, that
> I will do strongly before the sun and moon whatever inly rejoices
> me and the heart appoints.

The transcendentalist idea in this, of course, is that one must be true to
himself first and thus allow his true character to emerge. That supposed
character was always about to be fulfilled when it was awash in the kind
of ecstasy we find in Claudel's "Abandon" or Keats's "Ode." After his
first wife's death, Emerson was prepared to find that abandonment in the
soul's return to the "Over-Soul." In other words, he placed his trust in
the harmony of nature. However, for Austin, the prototype for Dickinson's "supposed persons," nature was "other" and hostile. Rather than
be simply "part or parcel" of God, he wanted to become whole in the
here and how. He wanted so desperately to be God or God-like that he
shouted himself into a pillar of salt. He tried to take experience beyond
its limits – indeed, beyond the limits of nature. He declared his "Rubicon" and found himself in another "Cold Pastoral." Not quite out of
life, he was never really in it either, for total fulfillment required the
selection of one's own society. This *was* the final harmony of nature (as
Emerson – and Whitman – had discovered). It was the solitary self, the
one "singing in the West" because the East of every beginning was irrevocably lost in the spent illusions of a lifetime. Dickinson sought the
same independence and found it not in either soul or body, but in the
"Cold Pastoral" of the "mind alone."

Her poetry departs, therefore, from Emerson's and Whitman's in its
negative capability. Whereas their poetry stands up for the First Amend-
ment rights of the solitary self, hers negates that self in order to preserve
it. Emerson has taught that "there is properly no history, only biography," and Whitman had claimed to "contain multitudes." But this right
of free speech – the right to speak the mind of all humankind – was not
constitutionally protected in Dickinson's jurisprudence. It was instead
muted in what another American poet had called "a still voice." Her
"thanatopsis" overrules the rooftop optimism of her precursors in the
American Renaissance. Faith was never her "invention." The self was
not only solitary but selfless, and representative of nothing more than its
own ecstatic moment in the continuous present. Emerson's persona may

have had the faith to believe that "all poetry was written before time was," and Whitman's may have thought he was speaking the word "primeval," but Dickinson's persona supposed nothing about the past and refused to invent a future. Everything depended on her – as it did for William Carlos Williams and other Dickinson disciples in the twentieth century – on the "emergency" of the present.

This relentless focus upon the present, however, does not deny the desire for an afterlife. Dickinson joins Emerson, Whitman, and every other great poet in this hope. Moreover, her microscopic accounting of the physical (what Williams called "thingness") reinforces her desire for something more. Elements of eighteenth-century rationalism can be found in her work as well as in that of the Transcendentalists: They all hoped the present harmony of nature signified a greater harmony or order. But Dickinson is an original American poet in her refusal to dwell in or even upon such a future. The "fair schoolroom of the sky" was one transfer and promotion her second story could not allow. For the elevation could commence only "When Time is over" (J. 193), and her second story had everything to do with time. She may have believed in "another sky" (J. 2) or thought human desire capable of overcoming *"space, or time!"* (J. 1), in her valentine's phase, but the poet who grew up to become simply and boldly "Dickinson" in many of her letters knew that – Thoreau to the contrary – time *was* an "ingredient" in every work of art. Time was the "Test of Trouble" (J. 686), and the "trouble" with Emily was that she was more interested in what the "Eclipse" revealed than in what it concealed.

For Thoreau's fictional artist of Kouroo in *Walden,* his art is perfect because time is omitted. But in actuality Thoreau never came any closer to finding his perfect staff than he came to finding his hound, bayhorse, or turtle dove. Nor did Dickinson, for a work of art was always penultimate and imperfect because time, or change, was its raison d'être. *Walden* was the second story, not the ultimate story. That was reserved for the "schoolroom" in the sky. And class there was not conducted by the poet, who worked almost exclusively with materials of this world, but by the schoolmaster, who, as Henry Adams tells us, was "employed to tell lies to little boys." They were not, of course, the lies that told the truth, but merely fables such as the one about the artist in the city of Kouroo or Thoreau's tall tale about a beautiful bug that came out of a dry leaf of an old table. These were tall tales, not true tales – untrue because they "ended" happily instead of with THE END. The real tall tale was happy and unending, too, but also true because it exaggerated the present instead of the future. There was no HAPPY ENDING because such a tale always ended in the middle, poised oxymoronically as the "still unravish'd bride" of experience.

The "mind alone" is the ultimate exaggeration. Dickinson followed

Emerson's advice of writing large her autobiography, but she stopped short of writing it "in colossal cipher." She stopped short of soul *searching*. If the existence of the mind provided an index for the metaphysical, she was nevertheless too busy with the present to care. She cast her lot with the Not-Me, her "divine Majority" instead of Whitman's "divine average." Defined by what it was not, its very negation was power. From her second story Dickinson could appreciate the duality. Life was a way of dying, but

> It was not Death, for I stood up,
> And all the Dead, lie down –
> It was not Night, for all the Bells
> Put out their Tongues, for Noon

The importance of this poem has been eclipsed by the critics' curiosity about the antecedent of "It" (generally thought to be "despair"), but the poem is really about life as seen from the second story. That is to say, its narrator, like that of "My Life Had Stood – a Loaded Gun" (J. 754), is another inanimate object – in this case, a statue:

> It was not Frost, for on my Flesh
> I felt Siroccos – crawl –
> Nor Fire – for just my Marble feet
> Could keep a Chancel, cool –

Statues represent the state of *having lived*. And frozen like one of Camille Claudel's sculptures, Dickinson's narrator surveys the life that is when she *was*. Dickinson sees life at its most statuesque: as the "Cold Pastoral" of the present. To appreciate this sudden-death quality of life is to feel, she tells us,

> As if my life were shaven,
> And fitted to a frame
> And could not breathe without a key
> And 'twas like Midnight, some –

"And – And – And!" At such moments the body inhales almost to the point of suffocation, for the moment of ecstasy is most like the moment of death:

> When everything that ticked – has stopped –
> And Space stares all around –
> Or Grisly frosts – first Autumn morns,
> Repeal the Beating Ground –
>
> But, most like Chaos – Stopless – cool –
> Without a Chance, or Spar –

Or even a Report of Land –
To justify – Despair.   (J. 510)

This is the "look of Agony" (J. 241) that she knows is real. It revealed a flawed and limping life ("This Me – that walks and works") and nothing else. It was the "mind alone" and it was the artist's only creation, for everything else – as Emerson said of poetry – had been written before time was. On the second story, Dickinson learned that she could never lose "as much but twice / And that was in the sod" (J. 49). One kept burying the corpse of his experience in a world that was finished as soon as it had begun.

NOTES

The notes that follow are keyed to the text by page number and catch phrase. Dickinson poems quoted or cited come from *Poems of Emily Dickinson*, ed. Thomas H. Johnson (Cambridge, Mass.: Harvard University Press, 1955), 3 vols., and are identified in the text by their assigned number (e.g., "J. 49").

PREFACE (pages ix–xiv)

Page ix

"corporeal friend": *Letters of Emily Dickinson*, ed. Thomas H. Johnson (Cambridge, Mass.: Harvard University Press, 1958), 2:460; hereafter cited as *Letters*.

"her 'Poets' ": *Letters*, 2:404.

Page x

"that walks alone": *Letters*, 2:460.

CHAPTER 1 (pages 1–13)

Page 1

"pseudo Sister": *Letters*, 3:716.

"God's Adversary": *Letters*, 3:755.

"It frightens me": quoted from Richard B. Sewall, *Life of Emily Dickinson* (New York: Farrar, Straus & Giroux, 1974), p. 178.

Page 2

"had a friend": *Letters*, 2:404

Page 3

"Presidents come and go": Sewall, *Life of Emily Dickinson*, p. 92.

"we three": Sewall, *Life of Emily Dickinson*, p. 180.

"loved in return": Sewall, *Life of Emily Dickinson*, p. 642.

"a passionate embrace": *Letters*, 3:733–4.

Page 4

"wildest word": *Letters*, 2:617.

"perfect soul-mate": Sewall, *Life of Emily Dickinson*, p. 183.

"she cannot pray": *Letters*, 2:421.

Page 5
"Burying Ground": *Letters*, 2:404.
"part or parcel": *Selections from Ralph Waldo Emerson: An Organic Anthology*, ed.
   Stephen E. Whicher (Boston: Houghton Mifflin, 1957), p. 24.
"loving bed-fellow": *Leaves of Grass: Comprehensive Reader's Edition*, ed. Harold
   W. Blodgett and Sculley Bradley (New York: Norton, 1965), p. 31.
Page 6
"lips in the West": *Letters*, 2:333.
Page 7
"as Mediator": *Jonathan Edwards: Representative Selections*, ed. Clarence H. Faust
   and Thomas H. Johnson (New York: Hill & Wang, 1962), p. 69.
"not directly to Eve": Margaret Homans, *Women Writers and Poetic Identity: Dor-
   othy Wordsworth, Emily Brontë, and Emily Dickinson* (Princeton, N.J.: Princeton University Press, 1980), p. 200.
Page 8
"syllable of Truth": *Letters*, 2:374.
Page 9
"knowing her fault": Sewall, *Life of Emily Dickinson*, p. 518.
"love so big": *Letters*, 2:391.
"time of her crisis": *Letters*, 2:250.
Page 10
"Dickinson's unrequited love": David Higgins, *Portrait of Emily Dickinson: The
   Poet and Her Prose* (New Brunswick, N.J.: Rutgers University Press, 1967),
   passim; and Ruth Miller, *The Poetry of Emily Dickinson* (Middletown, Conn.:
   Wesleyan University Press, 1968), *passim.*
"corporeal friend": *Letters*, 2:460.
"Miss Emily Grierson": *Collected Stories of William Faulkner* (New York: Vintage
   Books, 1977), p. 119.
Page 11
"tribute to . . . Jackson": *Poems of Emily Dickinson*, ed. Thomas H. Johnson
   (Cambridge, Mass.: Harvard University Press, 1955), 3:1103; hereafter cited
   as *Poems.*
Page 12
"Lunatics!": *Letters*, 2:576.
"Love's Adversary": *Letters*, 3:755.

CHAPTER 2 (pages 14–31)

Page 14
"Norcross girls": *Letters*, 3:906; and Martha Dickinson Bianchi, *Emily Dickinson
   Face to Face: Unpublished Letters with Notes and Reminiscences* (Boston: Hough-
   ton Mifflin, 1932), pp. xxii, 269.
"Mr. Bowles": *Letters*, 3:856.
Page 17
"amateur music": *Letters*, 2:347.
"no schoolboy's theme!": *Letters*, 2:328.

"little printed": *Walden and Civil Disobedience,* ed. Owen Thomas (New York: Norton, 1966), p. 75.

"here to regret": *T. S. Eliot: Collected Poems 1909–1962* (New York: Harcourt, Brace & World, 1963), p. 196.

Page 18

"until the age of fifteen": *Letters,* 2:475.

Page 19

"Strange things": *Poems,* 1:152–3.

"Vision to that of Wisdom": Jerome Loving, *Emerson, Whitman, and the American Muse* (Chapel Hill, N.C.: University of North Carolina Press, 1982), *passim.*

"a private fruit": *Selections from Ralph Waldo Emerson,* p. 272.

Page 20

"that will not dodge us": *Selections from Ralph Waldo Emerson,* pp. 256–7.

"psychosexual maturity": John Cody, *After Great Pain: The Inner Life of Emily Dickinson* (Cambridge, Mass.: Harvard University Press, 1971), p. 117.

Page 21

"morning star": *Walden and Civil Disobedience,* p. 221

Page 22

"an Eclipse": *Letters,* 2:404.

"an awful precipice": *Letters,* 1:31.

"childhood and adolescence": See Albert Gelpi, *Emily Dickinson: The Mind of the Poet* (Cambridge, Mass.: Harvard University Press, 1965), pp. 31–3.

"something so desolate": *Letters,* 1:94.

Page 23

"*boots,* and *whiskers*": *Letters,* 2:99.

"that old Chapel Aisle": See Kathleen E. Kier, "Only Another Suspension of Belief: Emily Dickinson's 'I've Heard an Organ Talk, Sometimes,' " *Massachusetts Studies in English,* 7–8 (1981), 18–27.

Page 24

"obsessive concern": Sewall, *Life of Emily Dickinson,* p. 198.

Page 25

"pseudo Sister": *Letters,* 3:716.

"sex in the subjunctive": Albert Gelpi, *The Tenth Muse: The Psyche of the American Poet* (Cambridge, Mass.: Harvard University Press, 1975), p. 249.

"the malignant reader": *Poems,* 1:180.

Page 26

"libidinous joys only": *Leaves of Grass,* p. 109.

"we exist": *Selections from Ralph Waldo Emerson,* p. 269.

"off to, Lady?": *Leaves of Grass,* p. 38.

"metaphorical penis": Sandra M. Gilbert and Susan Gubar, *The Madwoman in the Attic: The Woman and the Nineteenth-Century Literary Imagination* (New Haven, Conn.: Yale University Press, 1979), p. 3

Page 27

"in America's favor": *Emerson in His Journals,* ed. Joel Porte (Cambridge, Mass.: Harvard University Press, 1982), p. 22.

Page 28

"sad every morning": *Emerson in His Journals,* p. 142.

"barbaric yawp": *Leaves of Grass,* p. 89.

Page 29

"soup societies": *Letters of Herman Melville,* ed. Merrell R. Davis and William R.
Gilman (New Haven, Conn.: Yale University Press, 1960), p. 127.

"broken and in heaps": *Selections from Ralph Waldo Emerson,* p. 55.

Page 30

"moonless night": *Emerson in His Journals,* p. 54.

"laryngeal patterns": Edward Sapir, *Culture, Language and Personality* (Berkeley:
University of California Press, 1956), p. 3.

Page 31

"new wakefulness of words": Mutlu Konuk Blasing, "Whitman's 'Lilacs' and
the Grammars of Time," *Publications of the Modern Language Association of
America* 97 (1982), 32.

CHAPTER 3 (pages 32–48)

Page 32

"could not stop for Death": See Clark Griffith, *The Long Shadow: Emily Dickinson's Tragic Poetry* (Princeton, N.J.: Princeton University Press, 1964), p. 25.

"as a *lawyer"*: *Years and Hours of Emily Dickinson,* ed. Jay Leyda (New Haven,
Conn.: Yale University Press, 1960), 1:178.

Page 33

"the apparent victim": *Billy Budd, Sailor (An Inside Narrative),* ed. Harrison Hay-
ford and Merton Sealts, Jr. (University of Chicago Press, 1962), p. 103.

Page 34

"age of twenty-five": *Letters of Herman Melville,* p. 130.

"alike and numb": *Letters,* 2:404.

Page 35

"Prescott's 'Circumstance' ": *Letters,* 2:404.

"why I write – so": *Letters,* 2:405.

"Let Emily sing": *Letters,* 2:421.

Page 36

"terror – since September": *Letters,* 2:404.

"Frazer Stearns": *Letters,* 2:386.

"gained a splendid victory": *Civil War Letters of George Washington Whitman,* ed.
Jerome Loving (Durham, N.C.: Duke University Press, 1975), p. 46.

"will never be written": *Walt Whitman: Prose Works 1892,* ed. Floyd Stovall (New
York: New York University Press, 1963), 1:117.

Page 37

"big heart": *Letters,* 2:397.

"excels my Piano": *Letters,* 2:404.

"fresh confidence": Sewall, *Life of Emily Dickinson,* p. 550.

"gingham or no": *Leaves of Grass,* p. 35.

"disgraceful": *Letters,* 2:404.

Page 39

"at Summer's full": Sewall, *Life of Emily Dickinson,* pp. 552–3.

Page 41

"specimens of verse": *Years and Hours of Emily Dickinson,* 2:55.

"*My* business": *Letters,* 2:413.

Page 42

"only Kangaroo": *Letters*, 2:412.

"Firmament to Fin": *Letters*, 2:408.

"Verse is alive?": *Letters*, 2:403.

"grandmothers": Barbara Antonia Clark Mossberg, *Emily Dickinson: When the Poet Is a Daughter* (Bloomington: Indiana University Press, 1982), p. 43.

Page 43

"my nerve power": *Letters*, 2:476.

"every-day comradeship": *Letters*, 2:74–6.

"Yesterday mean": *Letters*, 2:412.

Page 45

"unanchored tropism": David Porter, *Dickinson: The Modern Idiom* (Cambridge, Mass.: Harvard University Press, 1981), p. 195, *passim*.

Page 46

"second 'Master' letter": *Letters*, 2:374.

Page 47

"Vesuvian face": See Robert Weisbuch, *Emily Dickinson's Poetry* (University of Chicago Press, 1975), pp. 26–39.

"carriage holds not only": See Griffith, pp. 128–9.

CHAPTER 4 (pages 49–65)

Page 49

"Father Emerson": Richard Eberhart, *Collected Poems 1930–1976* (New York: Oxford University Press, 1976), p. 293.

"Christmas in Bethlehem": *Letters*, 3:804.

"Hearts, not flowers": *Letters*, 3:842.

"Trundle-Beds": *Letters*, 3:853.

"woods to play": *Letters*, 3:894.

"Nervous prostration": *Letters*, 3:802.

Page 50

"shocked and grieved her": *Letters*, 2:798.

"original relation": *Selections from Ralph Waldo Emerson*, p. 21.

Page 51

"outward and upward": Charles R. Anderson, *Emily Dickinson's Poetry; Stairway of Surprise* (New York: Holt, Rinehart, 1960), p. 37.

"ecstasy of living": *Letters*, 2:474.

Page 52

"pseudo Sister": *Letters*, 3:375.

Page 53

"controlling influences": Sewall, *Life of Emily Dickinson*, p. 197.

"Shakespeare": *Letters*, 3:733.

" 'belle' of Amherst": *Letters*, 1:13.

"mother . . . she never had": *Letters*, 2:475.

"just 'Sue' ": *Letters*, 2:379–80.

Page 54

"stimulus of Loss": *Letters*, 2:489.

"taught me – poverty!": *Letters*, 2:400

Page 55
"frolicsome gayety": *Letters of Emily Dickinson,* ed. Mabel Loomis Todd (Boston: Roberts Brothers, 1894), p. v.

Page 57
"mind and matter": *Writings of William James,* ed. John J. McDermott (University of Chicago Press, 1967), p. xliii.

Page 58
"Benjamin Franklin Newton": George Frisbie Whicher, *This Was a Poet: A Critical Biography of Emily Dickinson* (Cambridge, Mass.: Harvard University Press, 1939), p. 92.

Page 59
"You see I remember": *Letters,* 2:401.
" 'afoot' with her vision": *Leaves of Grass,* p. 61.

Page 60
"must banish me": *Letters,* 2:412.
"Representative of [her] Verse": *Letters,* 2:412.
"Sue 'proud' of her": *Letters,* 2:380.
"Jackson and others": Sewall, *Life of Emily Dickinson,* p. 580.

Page 61
"Longfellow's *Kavanagh*": Sewall, *Life of Emily Dickinson,* p. 164.
"little Force explodes": *Letters,* 2:414.

Page 62
"naughty little girl": Mossberg, *When the Poet Is a Daughter,* p. 56.
"Daisy knows": *Letters,* 2:391.

Page 64
"anticlimactic nature of death": Anderson, *Emily Dickinson's Poetry,* p. 232.
"skill of life": *Letters,* 2:504.

Page 65
"Gilbert's sweet command": *Letters,* 3:803.
"As to you Life": *Leaves of Grass,* p. 87.
"wing'd purposes": *Leaves of Grass,* p. 40.

CHAPTER 5 (pages 66–83)

Page 69
"Credibility's presumption": See Sharon Cameron, *Lyric Time: Dickinson and the Limits of Genre* (Baltimore, Md.: Johns Hopkins University Press, 1979), p. 71.
"master *and* subject": *Plato: The Republic* (New York: Penguin Books, 1974), p. 201.

Page 70
"Circumference": *Letters,* 2:412.
"my robust soul": *Leaves of Grass,* p. 81.

Page 73
"the power to die": See Cameron, *Lyric Time,* p. 69.

page 74
"by a pistol shot": *Poems,* 2:629.

Page 75

"festive comedies": C. L. Barber, *Shakespeare's Festive Comedies* (Princeton, N.J.: Princeton University Press, 1972), *passim*.

"how to grow up": *Letters*, 1:241.

Page 76

"personal existence": Jack Henry Abbott, *In the Belly of the Beast: Letters from Prison* (New York: Random House, 1981), p. 101.

Page 77

"huge first Nothing": *Leaves of Grass*, p. 81.

Page 78

"nescessity": *Manuscript Books of Emily Dickinson*, ed. R. W. Franklin (Cambridge, Mass.: Harvard University Press, 1981), 2:1195.

Page 79

"an aged man": *Collected Poems of W. B. Yeats* (New York: Macmillan, 1956), p. 191.

"psychic assets liquid": Lewis Heyde, *The Gift: Imagination and the Erotic Life of Property* (New York: Random House, 1979), pp. 167–70.

Page 81

"The Snake": *Poems of Emily Dickinson*, 2:713.

"mere sense of living": *Letters*, 2:474.

Page 82

"sent Dickinson a picture": Sewall, *Life of Emily Dickinson*, p. 612.

"pathetic counterfeits": *Letters*, 2:479.

CHAPTER 6 (pages 84–102)

Page 84

"ever 'married' ": William H. Shurr, *The Marriage of Emily Dickinson: A Study of the Fascicles* (Lexington: University of Kentucky Press, 1983), *passim*.

"Tomahawk": *Letters*, 1:392.

"no right to intrude": *Letters*, 2:392.

"fellow sufferer": Sewall, *Life of Emily Dickinson*, p. 459. For the most recent arguments for Wadsworth as Dickinson's "lover," see Shurr, *Marriage of Emily Dickinson;* and Vivian R. Pollak, *Emily Dickinson: The Anxiety of Gender* (Ithaca, N.Y.: Cornell University Press, 1984).

Page 85

"or her own selves": *Letters*, 2:473.

"Northwest Passage": Jean McClure Mudge, *Emily Dickinson & the Image of Home* (Amherst: University of Massachusetts Press, 1975), pp. 85, 88.

Page 87

"faces of men and women": *Leaves of Grass*, p. 87.

"Dickinson's lover as God": Shurr, *Marriage of Emily Dickinson*, p. 75.

Page 88

"lonely & rigorous books": *Letters*, 2:473.

Page 89

Pollak, *Anxiety of Gender*, p. 42.

"rational happiness": Sewall, *Life of Emily Dickinson*, p. 49.

Page 90
"care for thought": *Letters*, 2:404.
"Two Editors": *Letters*, 2:404–5.
Page 91
"Jackson and her Indians": See Jackson's *A Century of Dishonor* (1881) and *Ramona* (1884).
"confidence in fraud": *Letters*, 2:415.
"Mrs. Adam": *Letters*, 1:24.
Page 92
"recent critical fantasy": Shurr, *Marriage of Emily Dickinson*, p. 170 *passim*.
Page 93
"in battles": *Early Lectures of Ralph Waldo Emerson*, ed. Robert E. Spiller and Wallace E. Williams (Cambridge, Mass.: Harvard University Press, 1972), 3:29.
"mere sense": *Letters*, 2:474.
Page 94
"eye treatment": Martin Want and Richard B. Sewall, " 'Eyes Be Blind, Heart Be Still': A New Perspective on Emily Dickinson's Eye Problem," *New England Quarterly*, 52 (1979), 400–6.
"saved my Life": *Letters*, 2:460.
"and long more": *Letters*, 2:459.
Page 95
"before time was": *Selections from Ralph Waldo Emerson*, p. 224.
Page 97
"Austin is alleged": Millicent Todd Bingham, *Ancestor's Brocades: The Literary Debut of Emily Dickinson* (New York: Harper, 1945), p. 233; and *Years and Hours of Emily Dickinson*, 1:328.
"never visited his grave": *Letters*, 2:526, 538.
"dry & speechless": *Letters*, 2:475.
Page 99
"busy with his Briefs": *Letters*, 2:404.
"Let Emily sing": *Letters*, 2:421.
Page 100
"home itself": *Letters*, 2:538.

CHAPTER 7 (pages 103–13)

Page 103
"origin of all poems": *Leaves of Grass*, pp. 31, 29.
Page 104
"closest earthly friend": *Letters*, 3:737.
"Nervous prostration": *Letters*, 3:802.
Page 105
"scholars' idle times": *Selections from Ralph Waldo Emerson*, p. 68.
Page 107
"Women talk": *Letters*, 2:473–4; and *Selections from Ralph Waldo Emerson*, p. 394.

"Thoreau is alleged": Walter Harding, *Days of Henry David Thoreau* (New York: Knopf, 1962), p. 464.

Page 110

"the heart appoints": *Selections from Ralph Waldo Emerson*, p. 160.

"part or parcel": *Selections from Ralph Waldo Emerson*, p. 24.

"singing in the West": *Leaves of Grass*, p. 16.

"a still voice": "Thanatopsis" in *Poems of William Cullen Bryant*, ed. Louis Untermeyer (New York: Heritage Press, 1947), pp. 10–11.

Page 111

"lies to little boys": *The Education of Henry Adams*, ed. Ernest Samuels (Boston: Houghton Mifflin, 1973), p. 9.

Page 112

"divine Majority": See Shira Wolosky, *Emily Dickinson: A Voice of War* (New Haven, Conn.: Yale University Press, 1984), p. 129.

INDEX OF POEMS DISCUSSED

GENERAL INDEX